BIM Demystified
An architect's guide to
Building Information Modelling/
Management (BIM)

2nd edition

Steve Race DipArch(Dist) ARB, RIBA

RIBA ⦚ **Publishing**

Dedication

I would like to dedicate this book to my family who have never really understood what I do, but have always supported my doing it.

Cover of BS 1192:2007 reproduced with permission © British Standards Institution (BSI)

Extracts from JCT Constructing Excellence contract reproduced with permission of Sweet and Maxwell publishers © The Joint Contracts Tribunal Limited

© Steve Race, 2013

First published by RIBA Publishing, 15 Bonhill Street, London EC2P 2EA

ISBN 978 1 85946 520 2
Stock code 81044

The right of Steve Race to be identified as the Author of this Work has been asserted in accordance with the Copyright, Designs and Patents Act 1988.

British Library Cataloguing in Publication Data
A catalogue record for this book is available from the British Library.

Commissioning Editor: James Thompson, Sarah Busby
Project Editor: Kate Mackillop
Designed and typeset by Phil Handley
Printed and bound by Butler Tanner & Dennis Ltd, Frome and London, UK
Cover design: Phil Handley

While every effort has been made to check the accuracy and quality of the information given in this publication, neither the Author nor the Publisher accept any responsibility for the subsequent use of this information, for any errors or omissions that it may contain, or for any misunderstandings arising from it.

RIBA Publishing is part of RIBA Enterprises Ltd, www.ribaenterprises.com

Acknowledgements

First and foremost to Michael Woodcock, my tutor at Hull School of Architecture, for having the courage and foresight to support one student along a new and unknown voyage of discovery with computers in architecture.

To the two Arschavir brothers both unfortunately deceased now, Arto and Ara. Arto was the Head of School at Hull School of Architecture, and Ara the Regional Works officer at Oxford Regional Health Authority. Although neither understood a single IT concept at that time they had the faith to provide a context, one in academia and the other in the public sector, for a new form of expertise to flourish in architecture.

Finally, to Gerald West, a partner in Fitzroy Robinson, who was one of the few senior managers who understood and was willing to back new business propositions offered by IT in architecture and construction.

100617066
720'
113
RAC

Contents

	Foreword to 2nd edition by Paul Fletcher RIBA	11
	Preface	13
SECTION 1	**BIM: THE MOVEMENT NOT THE ACRONYM**	**15**
	Did you know you might already be using BIM?	15
	Beware the acronym	16
	Modelling or management?	16
	BIM in the USA and UK	17
	The influence of the recession	20
	The influence of the Government initiative	21
	The global market and competition	21
	Tired with the old ways of working?	22
	SMEs can lead the way	22
	An emerging understanding	23
	BIM is an approach to creating and managing information	24
	The acronym has outgrown its usefulness	24
	Summary – BIM: the movement not the acronym	26
SECTION 2	**THE WHO, WHAT AND WHEN OF APPLYING BIM**	**27**
	How far will BIM be applied among project team members?	27
	How much of project life cycle will BIM cover?	28
	What range of information can BIM cover?	29
	It's usually a struggle	30
	BIM – a state of mind	31
	Summary – The who, what and when of applying BIM	34
SECTION 3	**BIM INGREDIENTS**	**35**
	2D 'drawings'	35
	One software platform	37
	Objects	38
	— What is an object?	38
	— The new design team member	39
	Parametrics	40
	Intranets, extranets, portals and clouds	41
	— The basics	41
	— What else do portals offer?	42
	— Problems with portals	43
	— Clouds	44

	— IaaS – Infrastructure as a Service	44
	— PaaS – Platform as a Service	45
	— SaaS – Software as a Service (also known as 'On-demand Software')	46
	Standards	46
	— BS 1192 (2007)	47
	— CI/SfB	47
	— UNICLASS	49
	Mix your own ingredients	49
	Summary – Where does BIM come from?	50
SECTION 4	**THE BUSINESS CASE FOR BIM**	**51**
	Whose business case?	52
	Can we afford it?	52
	What effect will it have on salary levels?	53
	How much do we invest in training?	54
	Training in information management	55
	Summary – The business case for BIM	56
SECTION 5	**BIM IN THE OFFICE**	**57**
	A question of scale	57
	The small scale office	57
	The medium scale office	58
	The large scale office	59
	Office methodology – how do we change our working practices?	59
	Office – the partner/director/CAD user divide	60
	Summary – BIM in the office	60
SECTION 6	**BIM WITHIN THE PROJECT**	**61**
	Technology or methodology?	61
	Summary – BIM within the project	62
SECTION 7	**WHAT NEW BUSINESS OPPORTUNITIES COME WITH BIM?**	**63**
	BIM as an investment	63
	Do we charge extra fees?	63
	Add more value using forms of appointment	64
	A step further	65
	Beware the Code of Conduct	65
	Summary – What new business opportunities come with BIM?	66

SECTION 8	**WILL OUR CLIENTS WANT BIM?**	**67**
	Is the client suitable and willing to adopt BIM?	67
	What are the benefits for the client?	68
	Are there costs to the client? – yes and no	69
	A new stimulus from Government	69
	Education on both sides of the counter	69
	Summary – Will our clients want BIM?	71

SECTION 9	**BIM IN THE SUPPLY CHAIN**	**73**
	The supply chain contributes a significant amount of information	73
	Engaging the supply chain	74
	The product supplier's dilemma (specification versus contractor buying cheapest)	75
	BIM education in the supply chain	75
	Summary – BIM in the supply chain	76

SECTION 10	**HOW DO WE IMPLEMENT BIM?**	**77**
	BIM metrics – choosing the individual	77
	BIM metrics – choosing the company	79
	— Champions	80
	— Policy	81
	— Experience	81
	— Technology and information standards	81
	— Flexibility	81
	— Teamwork	82
	— Innovation	82
	— Openness	82
	— If things go wrong – don't blame	82
	— Contracts	83
	BIM metrics – auditing the project team	83
	— The team comes together	84
	— Audit the team	84
	Facilitating the team	85
	Audit the process	85
	Audit roles and responsibilities	87
	Audit software	88
	— What's your version?	89
	Audit information conventions	90
	— Exchanging Information	92
	— What sort of information?	92
	— How do we exchange information?	93

— Direct proprietary links   93
— Public exchange formats   94
— And that horrible, foreboding but much used word, interoperability   94
Now you know your BIM environment   95
Post metrics – a convergence plan   95
— Locating information so that it fits together better   96
— Precision   98
— Where, who and what?   99
— Things get a little more complicated   100
What might be   103
Defining BIM Processes   103
— 1 BIM strategic planning   103
— 2 BIM development and implementation   104
— 3 BIM programme management   104
— 4 BIM information preparation and review   104
— 5 BIM input   105
— 6 BIM change   105
— 7 BIM focusing/discipline   106
— 8 BIM information risk management   106
Defining BIM roles – small and large office   106
— BIM Director   107
— BIM Manager   107
— BIM Focus/Discipline Group Manager   108
— BIM Author   108
— BIM Technologist   108
— BIM Support   108
— BIM HR Manager   109
AIA Document E202–2008 (AIA 2008)   109
Summary – How do we implement BIM?   112

SECTION 11   BIM IN A COLLABORATIVE LEGAL CONTEXT   **113**
Islands of contract   113
Collaborative contracts   113
Summary – BIM in a collaborative legal context   116

SECTION 12   BIM AS AN AGENT FOR CULTURAL CHANGE   **117**
Social technology compared with architectural and construction
technology   117
Summary – BIM as an agent for cultural change   118

SECTION 13   GOVERNMENT BIM   **119**

Launch of a nationwide initiative   119

The importance of the 28 February 2013 documents

(PAS 1192, COBie, CIC BIM Protocol, RIBA Plan of Work 2013)   119

— PAS 1192 Demystified   120

— COBie demystified   122

— BIM Protocol demystified   123

— The RIBA Plan of Work 2013   124

The BIM Regional Hubs and special interest groups   126

— The Hubs have several aims   126

Government Soft Landings BIM requirements   128

Summary – Government BIM   131

SECTION 14   BIM IN EDUCATION   **133**

The importance of education   133

The current state of BIM in higher education   134

Integration is the keynote in education   135

Summary – BIM in education   136

SECTION 15   WHERE WILL BIM GO IN THE FUTURE?   **137**

The political landscape   137

— Eliminate the rhetoric   138

— Outcomes   138

— Business proposition   139

— Other agencies   140

The cultural landscape   140

The technological future   141

— The immediate future   141

— Clever product information   142

— BIMs and BEMs   142

— Waiting for inventions   143

— Google – the sleeping giant for architecture and construction?   144

BIM in the future: security and virtuality   146

— Francis Maude's cyber security statements and policy   147

— The hacking threat and BIM   148

Big Data and virtual agents   149

Summary – Where will BIM go in the future?   154

Conclusion   155

INDEX   **157**

Foreword to 2nd edition

Steve Race was in many ways one of the earliest pioneers of what we now call BIM. He was using information modelling technologies whilst I was still at school; as a university student the work of D'Arcy Race was an early inspiration for my own journey into the world of information modelling, BIM and beyond...

Over the past few years BIM has become one of the most hotly debated and promoted issues within the construction industry. Everywhere you look you are bombarded: by software vendors, industry evangelists, and most significantly the government, who are mandating BIM Level 2 by 2016. All want to either sell you their technology, tell you how to work or extol the virtues of BIM. Common to all is the pervasive sense of bemusement and confusion that has been triggered in the industry: what really is BIM and what does it mean to me, my colleagues, my clients?

This is where this book excels: rather than pushing specific technologies or dictating how we should work it provides architects and fellow professionals with a rational and clear context in which they can begin their own journey into new and better ways of working. It explains where BIM has come from and how many of us are in some way doing it already – even if we did not previously realise it!

In the first edition of this book Steve demystified the whole concept of BIM, placing it firmly in the context of collaborative information-driven design, construction and operation. In this second edition he expands the narrative deeper into the supply chain, explains HM Government approach to BIM and the critical need for BIM in education. But where this edition is so relevant is when it looks to the future. Based on evidence given in the preceding chapters it concludes by setting the scene for a BIM evolution, through social media, Big Data and virtualisation. Surely the basis from which a 21st century built environment industry can deliver true excellence in built outcomes.

Paul Fletcher RIBA
Chair, RIBA Construction Strategy Group

Preface

This guide is aimed at the vast majority of people in mainstream practice. It is intended to offer an easygoing explanation of a subject which could be swamped by technical jargon and deluged with spin. There is some technology expressed in a form which the purists might find hard to swallow. Hopefully, for those for whom technology is not the main priority, some essential ideas of Building Information Modelling have been described in a digestible form. The guide takes a wider view of BIM encompassing business opportunity, the architect's code of conduct, cultural issues and the necessity for better legal arrangements to underpin BIM. The book addresses BIM from the point of view of architectural practice as opposed to a technological perspective.

Building Information Modelling, like many other topics in architecture and construction offers advantages; however, it requires a shift in attitude if its benefits are to be obtained. With any luck this book will provide a straightforward representation of the concepts involved and allow individuals at all levels in an architectural practice to build a firmer understanding and wider application of BIM. The book aims to bring together both strategists and technologists within architectural businesses to form improved and more valuable, in every sense of the word, propositions for built environment interventions.

SECTION 1
BIM: the movement not the acronym

Did you know you might already be using BIM?

Initiatives to establish better practice within architecture and construction appear with rapid succession. Improved integration, co-operative working and newer forms of contractual arrangements offer the prospect of changing the way interventions in the built environment are made. Architects are primarily trained as designers; many other activities and skills are needed to bring their ideas to fruition.

The current interest surrounding the phenomenon known as BIM simply reminds us that different attitudes, techniques and relationships come along from time to time to make us think about the way we manage our information. Since time immemorial architects have created information to express their intentions to other members of the design team. They have produced and communicated information in some form whether it be scribing simple depictions in sand, on papyrus, parchment, paper or today's modern complex and ubiquitous electronic forms.

For thousands of years an architect had a relatively close relationship with the craftsmen who created the final artefact. Communicating information was a comparatively straightforward and personal activity and the form and pace of the development of information communication was largely in the hands of the architect and the immediate team of artisans. Today the situation is radically different. Alongside their primary design skills, architects have to take on board information creation and communication in a way that previous generations never had to. On the one hand the internet has placed more and more information at our disposal. On the other, architects have to be increasingly vigilant in obtaining and filtering the information they require in a more litigious atmosphere. The information they themselves generate is subject to immense scrutiny by all members of the immediate and extended project team. Commercial clients are even more hyper-critical.

Architects often make decisions, sometimes wrongly, based on too little or too much information and almost always on information that is not integrated. To use information in better ways does not require architects to dispense with any of their existing skills, simply to think differently about the way they exercise them. Architects have been using BIM from the very first time information was exchanged in order to get something built. This book looks at some of the ingredients that influence the creation of information by architects and gives a framework for improvement. There is no need to believe that BIM is something entirely new and different. We, as architects, simply have to ask ourselves how we can produce information better and in a less adversarial environment.

Beware the acronym

BIM is one of the most recent acronyms to appear in the world of architecture and construction. The timing of its first appearance is difficult to establish. America claims its origination in 2002 as a means of describing virtual design, construction and facilities management. Various groups around the world were using the acronym at about the same time but with different meanings. BIM has already fallen into the same use, abuse and misuse that CAD, CADD and CADFM did. At best these acronyms provided a rough guide to what was being discussed; at worst they led to endless debate on whether the 'D' stood for design or drafting or drawing, a debate which produced nothing of practical relevance.

Equivalent problems of interpretation exist for BIM. Individual letters conjure up images in each person's mind. 'B', Building; for some this might mean an envelope and everything within it, for others the 'B' may connote a wider view of a building and its surroundings; infrastructures and landscaping for example. The word building is somewhat restrictive in conjuring up a broader range of considerations; it may not tell us anything about policies, assumptions, strategic decisions, brief content, user assessment, supply chains, regulation or recycling sustainability. Are all these to be implied and imagined from a meagre starting point of 'building'? 'I', Information, is quite straightforward if taken at face value and is probably the most important word represented within the acronym. The 'M' is interpreted in two quite different ways; model/modelling or management.

Modelling or management?

BIM is both an activity and a thing. The verb does not tell us who is doing the building modelling or the noun what the model contains. Does the activity simply imply the individual designer, the immediate team in the individual design practice, the wider project team and supply chains, or all of these, plus users and maintenance personnel? Does the verb cover information creation, collection, updating, archiving collating, co-ordinating, validating or sharing? Does the model include 2D graphics, 3D graphics, intelligent objects, parametrics and all physical and electronic forms of non-graphic information?

In this context model/modelling can be taken to mean a representation to a smaller scale, a simulation of how something works, or a representation of something in a different form or media to the original. Using model/modelling as the respective noun or verb gives a range of possibilities from the static to the dynamic, which is acceptable when thinking of information in project life cycle. Interpreting 'M' as management gives a far more potent and all-encompassing notion of what the acronym is really intended to portray. Management, among other things, implies planning, organising, resourcing and controlling not simply the information that is required on a project, but the people who create and combine it to produce the finished built environment artefact.

Management is an essential ingredient in translating often complex and disparate information from a wide variety of sources into an organised whole that is continually updated and used by the project team. The way information is managed determines the confidence people have in it and the effect it has on success and profitability for all concerned. There are more profound and far reaching implications interpreting 'M' as management rather than model or modelling. This is far the better option, in that it is currently contributing to wider discussions and initiatives about improved co-operation between project team members. Taking the letters at face value produces an impression of the architectural and construction world that falls far short of the real complex issue of information creation and management in any project life cycle, whatever its scale.

Project Information Management (PIM) or Project Lifecycle Information Management (PLIM) may have been more helpful and more indicative of the intention to form a comprehensive information package that represents the life of a facility. Any acronym probably suffers from inadequacy of implication or completeness of meaning, so there will be many happy hours of friendly debate on just what is meant by BIM.

BIM in the USA and UK

One of the most strategic documents on BIM and collaborative supported IT issued anywhere in the world to date is the 'National 3D-4D-BIM Program, additional BIM Guide Series', issued by the Office of the Chief Architect, Public Buildings Service of the US General Services Administration in Washington. The challenge has been accepted and many states have announced initiatives based on the central policy statement, for example the State of Wisconsin has declared that all its state-funded facilities over the capital value of $5m will use BIM techniques. Moreover the General Services Administration (GSA) has offered its own definition of BIM as follows. 'Building Information Modeling is the development and use of a multi-faceted computer software data model to not only document a building design, but to simulate the construction and operation of a new capital facility or a recapitalised (modernised) facility. The resulting Building Information Model is a data-rich, object-based, intelligent and parametric digital representation of the facility. From this, views appropriate to various users' needs can be extracted and analysed to generate feedback and improvement of the facility.'

This is a courageous statement that embraces most modern IT concepts in architectural and construction software, namely objects and parametrics. The scope is wide enough to allow a range of BIM interpretations from the most humble 2D 'drawing database' to the most sophisticated modern technology. As if this was not enough the American Institute of Architects has published *AIA Document E202–2008, Building Information Modeling Protocol Exhibit*. The document provides a very worthwhile proforma to assist project teams in establishing their methodology for implementing a project based on BIM principles. It offers a definition of BIM ('A Building Information Model is a digital representation of the physical and functional characteristics of the Project and is referred to in this Exhibit as the "Model(s)", which may be used herein to describe a Model Element, a single Model or multiple Models used in the aggregate. "Building Information Modelling" means the process and technology used to create the Model'). It provides the following section headings which the project team then complete for themselves:

- An opportunity to set out model management responsibilities both in the immediate and longer term.
- The level to which any element in the BIM should be modelled.
- The author of any element.
- The uses to which the model can reliably be deployed.

The document is by no means exhaustive in what a project team might need for a comprehensive implementation of BIM, but what it does give is a valuable framework which, with the right attitudes from team players, would significantly lift the level of information creation and management, and thus enhance advantage all round. The AIA document would form a natural partnership with the relatively new Joint Contracts Tribunal (JCT) Constructing Excellence form of contract. This contract is an innovative statement by the JCT and represents a paradigm shift from an adversarial to a collaborative form of contract. It provides for the annexation of a Project Protocol which could take the AIA document or a development of it as its basis. It is a quasi-legal document. Its power is not its legal bearing or its technological depth; the monumental consideration is that it is produced by a powerful institutional body like the AIA.

It is architects claiming some ground for themselves rather than allowing other disciplines and project team players to usurp architects, as has so often happened in the past. More significant is the fact that these documents and proclamations come from incredibly significant and influential practices within the USA. This in itself is a major boost to the adoption and spread of BIM. Having said that, many of the examples and case studies generated by the USA exhibit no more than the customary struggle to manage and exchange information born out of the use of a proliferation of systems that can be found on most medium and large scale projects.

Pre 2010 the USA led the way in evangelising about BIM at any level. Until the Government's chief advisor on construction, Paul Morrell, indicated in October 2010 that BIM would play a key part in Government procurement policy. Since then the UK has made significant strides in taking on the challenges implied by BIM procurement methods. This is evidenced by the publication in 2011 of a BIM Industry Working Group report on BIM, *BIM: Management for Value, Cost and Carbon Improvement*, in response to an invitation by the Cabinet Office to 'look at the construction and post-occupancy benefits of BIM for use in the UK building and infrastructure markets'.

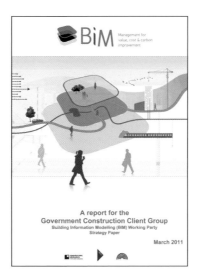

FIGURE 1.1 A report for the Government Construction Client Group. Building Information Modelling (BIM) Working Party Strategy Paper.

The report is symbolic. It has taken many years and many reports and much effort on behalf of small groups and individuals to eventually bring this to the notice of Government. The idea that information assets are both valuable to the client, whether public or private and whatever scale, but at the same time also represent a different way of working has been a long time in the realisation. If the Government client can lead the way in incorporating BIM methodologies into its procurement process then there could be a quantum shift in the way the UK construction industry conducts itself.

An attractive feature of this prospect is that a BIM outlook will be encouraged to percolate through all scales of practice. Mainstream architectural practices could take the opportunity to hone their BIM skills. There are major prizes to be won. The report champions newer forms of collaborative contract which is essential if project teams are to co-operate in a more comfortable legal environment. The danger is that a narrow concept such as BIM uses one software platform or convoluted technical standards required for information exchange which might prejudice those who have the procurement power. Whatever the connotation placed on the acronym, in this document it represents a powerful force for change, it should not be abused.

The influence of the recession

At the time of writing the most recent review by the Office for National Statistic shows that the economic output of the construction industry was in decline from Q1 2008 to Q2 2009. From then onwards there has been a steady recovery but the first quarter of 2012 was slower than equivalent quarters in 2010 and 2011.

In such stark economic times the hardship that private and public sector organisations and companies have encountered has encouraged a reappraisal of current work practices to seek out opportunities for improvement. Given few alternatives, small groups of individuals or entire local government departments have seen BIM as a possible solution to meeting the harsh realities of the recession.

In one architectural practice in Scotland for example a small group of people decided to implement their version of BIM. They demonstrated benefit to themselves and then took that to the senior managers in their practice. BIM was adopted further within the business and on more and more projects.

At another scale of operation a local authority department felt that because of Government cuts in budget the status quo could no longer exist. They too experimented with their version of BIM. They kept the experiment within the bounds of a single local authority department and out of the hands of the local politicians until they too demonstrated benefit to themselves. Then they went public.

Both these examples show how a smaller entity can demonstrate BIM advantage to itself. That entity establishes and owns the benefit whatever that might be. It could be financial, but there are other benefits such as job satisfaction, more value propositions to clients and unlocking poor decision points in company processes.

The old adage 'through adversity comes strength (and opportunity)' appears to be true in recessive times.

The influence of the Government initiative

The Government initiative on BIM since 2010 is perhaps one of the most profound policies the construction industry has ever seen. Sir Michael Latham in his 1994 report encouraged us to review our procurement and contractual relationships and advised us to engage in more partnering and collaboration. In 1998 Egan echoed these sentiments and emphasised integrated processes. Both did their bit but never has there been such a comprehensive geographical, inclusive, pan professional, supply chain outreaching initiative in the history of construction.

The launch of BIM Regional Hubs throughout England, Scotland, Wales and Northern Ireland has established a network of enthusiasm and co-operation that could revolutionise the way UK Construction Plc operates in future. The main aim of the Regional Hubs is to act as a two-way conduit between industry and the BIM Task Group in order to raise awareness of the Government Construction Strategy (GCS) relating to BIM at a local level throughout the UK.

The global market and competition

World population predictions appear to congregate around the seven billion plus mark by 2016. The market for construction projects therefore is set to expand drastically in the intervening period and beyond. The Joseph Rowntree Foundation points to a housing shortage of one million homes by the year 2022 in the UK context alone.

There are many reports showing the growth of the use of BIM in various countries, for example Richard Saxon CBE's *Growth Through BIM* report funded by the Department for Business, Innovation and Skills and carried out through the Construction Industry Council gives an excellent prognosis for the growth of BIM in the UK and internationally. However, given the indeterminate understanding of BIM it is hard to pinpoint what BIM means to the respondents within the survey and which BIM ingredients are being referred to. The individual percentages in one sense are therefore quite meaningless but all the surveys show an increase in BIM use, whatever that might mean, again adding grist to the mill as far as the adoption of BIM is concerned.

There is no doubt that BIM is being debated and implemented in some shape or form on a global basis, the most notable area of the globe of course being China. China is so enthusiastic about BIM that it has launched five national standards; although something of a contradiction in terms, this nevertheless illustrates the Chinese exuberance for embracing wholeheartedly all things Western and then excelling in their use or production.

Japan, the other technology-absorbing culture, appears to be lagging behind somewhat. Surveys show that although a large proportion of the Japanese construction industry is aware of BIM, its actual uptake of BIM is relatively slow according to a survey conducted by Globaltrade.net

Of course the main competition in BIM is between the UK and the USA. There probably is no definitive way of assessing who is in front in terms of adoption. Indeed, even if that mattered, the main point is that the usual jousting between the two countries progresses the BIM movement.

The UK obviously now feels its post-2010 efforts put it in the first division and that it can export its BIM expertise to Europe and beyond. Richard Saxon CBE's report mentioned above supports the view that the UK is in the lead. The Government's BIM initiative is the strongest statement any government has made and is supported by an unprecedented level of activity within the construction industry.

Tired with the old ways of working?

There is a growing feeling that the old adversarial ways of working are guilty of being the producers of the highest proportion of waste in the construction industry; higher than any materials or carbon inefficiencies can produce. Conflicting and complicated contracts, non-collaboration, claim chasing and a blame culture are examples of activities that generate wasted and costly effort.

Having said that, the forms of contract that could provide a more positive way forward appear to be lost in the background. For example the JCT Constructing Excellence contract. The average project team appears not to search out and seriously implement available co-operative legal contracts.

Experienced people are the ones who could take on newer forms of contract and use their experience to mould them into powerful new tools. There is a brave minority who are prepared to do this but many are held back by false assumptions and fear of the unfamiliar.

However, groups such as the BIM2050 group which represents the younger generation in the Government's BIM intiative display a wonderfully refreshing attitude towards an integrated approach and hopefully represent a future generation who can work together in better ways.

SMEs can lead the way

SMEs have one of the most remarkable opportunities in recent times. The Government's BIM initiative is a moment in time when their ability to be lean, mean and BIMkeen can put them in the driving seat. Currently there is a mood of opposites amongst SME's: some worry whether they can keep up with the big boys whereas some feel they can steal a march on them. The latter is the more likely.

It is true that large companies have perhaps more resource at their disposal, although times are hard for everybody. But they have their own bureaucracies and pockets of Luddites, sceptics and cynics whose outlook is difficult to change and who provide one of the biggest barriers to BIM change.

Most of the supply chain is composed of SME. The construction industry relies on them heavily. Many professional consultants, product producers, software and, today, apps creators tend to be relatively smaller companies (with some exceptions of course). They can adapt their expertise, products and software offerings far quicker than the proverbial oil tanker can change direction.

The BIM movement should mean that SMEs have never had it so good. The potential for growth for them is bounded only by their willingness to get involved.

An emerging understanding

Currently there is still no single, agreed explanation or definition of what BIM is. Printed material and software vendor spin could give the unsuspecting the impression that the concept is well understood and clear. Understanding exactly what is on offer has always been a problem since the dawn of time, when software systems were introduced to the architectural profession and the construction industry.

To some extent ambiguity and imprecision has encouraged cynicism and resistance to these systems and methodologies germinating and blossoming in a positive way that assists co-operative working. It is not unexpected therefore that BIM, like beauty, is in the eye of the beholder. Different project team professionals, stakeholders and practices have their own interpretations of BIM. The immediate past has seen the emergence of many definitions from both industry and academia. In the 1990s attempts at defining BIM included terms such as digital model, nD, project model, virtual prototyping, integrated project database, an electronic data model and a digital representation of a facility. None of these terms provided a satisfactory solution to the definition process and as soon as one definition emerged, another took its place with perhaps other factors being taken into account.

One thing is certain; these early attempts were predominantly technological in flavour. It was not until the noughties that the scope of BIM explanations became wider as the realisation dawned that BIM could potentially bring about transformations in the way clients, architects, constructors and facility users operated together. The following definition offered by Succar et al. (2007) and building on an earlier definition by Penttilä (2006) begins to indicate that BIM might have more than simply a technologically orientated interpretation. 'Building Information Modelling (BIM) is a set of interacting policies processes and technologies producing a methodology to manage the essential building design and project data in digital format throughout the building's life-cycle'.

Key words such as 'policies', 'processes', 'methodology' and 'manage' begin to change the landscape, indicating the potential for a wider interpretation of BIM. Further extrapolations of what BIM might include in the near future are knowledge sharing, process analysis and change, modifications to contractual bases and insurance sharing. The aspiration to work in a more co-operative way, as Egan and Latham advocated many years earlier, strikes at the very heart of the way the architectural profession in particular and the construction industry in general operates.

BIM is an approach to creating and managing information

So we see, BIM is not about an individual software platform, a particular industry standard or a form of contract. These are powerful devices that can be used to good effect at various levels and in many combinations. Software platforms and standards of various types can play a part but they can be as divisive as they are cohesive. It is the collective state of mind behind their use in any combination and at any level that determines the benefit.

In today's world information is king. Construction is perhaps one of the heaviest information producing industry sectors. Never have there been so many parties contributing information to the built, used and recycled product. BIM represents a realisation that information cannot be produced in silos whose contents rarely pay attention to their neighbour. BIM is a force for co-operation and teamwork. The important and far more potent idea is that the current interest in BIM provides the potential for a more positive and beneficial way of creating the information asset required for producing, managing and using the national building stock.

A significant point is that the principles behind a BIM approach to managing information are scalable. The ideas and techniques discussed in subsequent sections of this book are as applicable to the smaller practice as they are to the large scale, multi-disciplinary, multinational player. So far 'BIM' has been used as a working expression to cover many ideas. The rest of this book will delve into the world of BIM to help you dissect the techniques, processes and business considerations which you might find helpful in your own practice's approach to implementing BIM.

From the beginning of time architects have always created and communicated information.

The acronym has outgrown its usefulness

The hoo-ha surrounding BIM has now been going on for more than three years since Paul Morrell made his first declarations on BIM in 2010. Those years have seen a remarkable change in the mood towards BIM within the construction industry and all its associated professional bodies, trades and state organisations. The original emphasis on technology has been replaced and put into the context of better management of information in the construction industry and the wider cultural implications of producing a better information asset for the end user; something which should create benefit for all.

CAD managers have now made the transition to calling themselves BIM managers. BIM directors, BIM champions, BIM leaders and BIM experts have all emerged in the intervening period from 2010. Never has there been such imagination in inventing job titles and their respective role definitions.

Technology also made its presence felt, as it would. Small additions have been made to the acronym, additions which have significant technological implications. 'iBIM' or interoperable BIM has given a boost to the quest for more robust and reliable information exchanges between software systems of both a graphical and non-graphical nature. This is the case even though 'interoperability' has its own discussion on what it means and how it should be implemented.

'pBIM' or proprietary BIM enjoys a debate about data exchange standards that are open to all or owned by individuals or organisations (usually the software vendor). There are several other technological extensions to the BIM acronym but they only serve to further clutter and confuse the BIM landscape. Technological interpretations of 'BIM' generate interesting discussion amongst the 'techies' which will eventually lead to innovation, but this is not the priority for project people whose job is to use software and not create it.

Outside technology other letters of the alphabet have been added in front of 'BIM' to fuel the fires of confusion. iBIM can apparently also mean 'integrated BIM' a much more useful connotation for co-operative working. If information was managed well then it would automatically be integrated, co-ordinated, quality controlled and full team co-operation would be in place. There would be no need to qualify the acronym any further.

So as a consequence of much erudite debate since 2010 the acronym has at one level lost meaning, having been so devalued by an interminable mixture of microscopic analysis, literal meaning, dismissal by cynics or Luddites and wide ranging debate academic or otherwise.

On the other hand the scene is not all doom, gloom and meaningless banter. The acronym has reached a peak of provocation, instigating one of the most profound periods of rethinking in the history of construction. Irrespective of the differing interpretations of 'BIM', or whether you are a technologist or a practitioner, the construction industry is now engaged in one of the most fundamental appraisals of how BIM operates.

BIM as an acronym does not matter now. To discuss its meaning is in itself meaningless. But it does matter that people explain what BIM means to them and how the BIM ingredients explained in this book are perceived and used in combination in any project context.

Of paramount importance is that BIM now represents a movement towards better co-operation and operation with every facet of the construction industry. It is symbolic of a new way of thinking that should profoundly benefit the outcomes that the construction industry provides for the built environment.

▶ **SUMMARY**

BIM: the movement not the acronym

• Beware the BIM acronym.

• Decide what the acronym means to you – use this book to find out.

• BIM is not an individual software platform or industry standard.

• BIM is an approach to creating and managing information.

• The UK Government BIM initiative has been a historic moment for construction in the UK.

• Given the current inertia created for BIM, the UK is in a prominent global position.

• Confrontation, poor integration of teams and inadequate information management are beginning to look as if they belong in the past.

• There are enormous opportunities for SMEs provided they use their size and abilities to adapt and adopt quickly.

• The BIM acronym has served a good purpose but it is now time to move on.

• BIM now represents a movement for change towards a more co-operative way of working.

SECTION 2
The who, what and when of applying BIM

How far will BIM be applied among project team members?

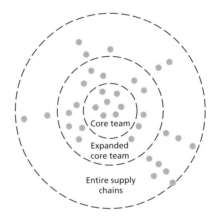

FIGURE 2.1 Extend BIM from the core team to the supply chains.

There are no bounds to how far BIM can be applied. As an attitude to information it can be applied as broadly as possible. Taking the RIBA work stages as a traditional and orthodox design process model but accepting there are many variations, then BIM might be used by the core team during stages 0 to 3 for example. The core team will usually be comprised of the immediate design consultants and the client.

These stages represent the formative period in the design process where client requirements, design assumptions and legal and regulatory parameters mould the design concept that will be created in detail and subsequently developed and constructed.

If this group of people can form an information alliance at this crucial stage then downstream thinking and design development will be far more effective and less prone to delay, confusion and claims. This is the key starting point for successful information management through the design and construction stages and beyond. The integration of thinking by this group will ameliorate the information base ready for input by other personnel as the project develops. The extended core team might involve the planning authorities, building control, CDM co-ordinator, party wall expert, any specialist survey material or the contractor outside a design and build type of context, all of whom could be briefed in the protocols of the particular approach taken to BIM. Their information could be absorbed straightaway or converted to a suitable format so that it formed an integral part of the project BIM.

Beyond that and in an ideal world, every complete supply chain would contribute to the BIM. Just-in-time inventory, lean construction methods and off-site fabrication would all benefit from the supply of well co-ordinated, quality controlled information from the BIM. BIM can offer supply chains better precision and reliability in measuring quantities and shorter potential tender times due to dependable information.

How much of project life cycle will BIM cover?

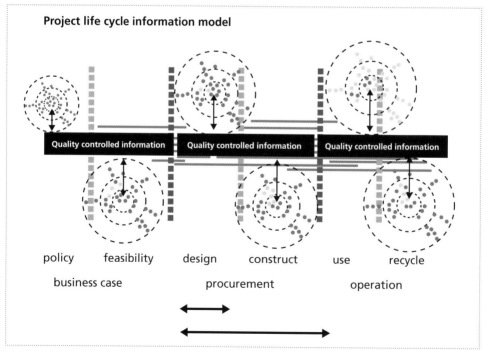

FIGURE 2.2 How much of project life cycle do you want to cover?

Generally the focus for the design team is traditionally pointed towards design and construction phases of a project. Earlier strategic and feasibility stages and the post-occupation stages can be neglected in a complete information picture of a project's life cycle. Somebody else has usually made a strategic set of decisions prior to the design and construction phases. This is true no matter what scale of project is being undertaken. For example, at the beginning of a project life cycle even the domestic home owner evaluates their family finances and makes a mortgage choice. At the other end of the scale very large projects may have had many and varied inputs to the decision to build; investment possibilities, population surveys, extensive user consultations and governmental input are all examples of strategic thinking before embarking on a built project.

Post construction, other parties become involved in generating information about the built facility; for example, users, maintainers, property managers and ultimately demolition experts. For some types of facility this onward phase produces more information than the original design construction period. Indeed for many practices information produced then, together with the as-built set, becomes an extremely valuable practice asset. BIM can be employed in any phase, the sooner the better, but it needs to be structured carefully at the outset and quality controlled rigorously through all phases.

What range of information can BIM cover?

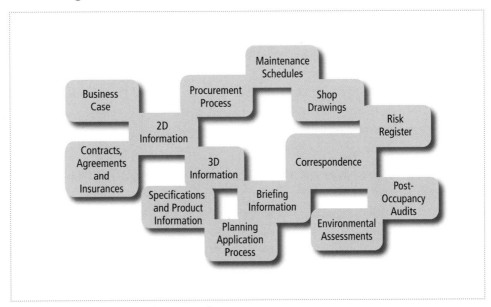

FIGURE 2.3 Typical types of project information.

BIM does not discriminate between the types of information that can be considered. Usually the emphasis is on graphic information; however non-graphic information is equally important when considering any form of information management. Contract, risk registers, all forms of correspondence, specification documents, manufacturers' technical information, reactive and preventive maintenance schedules could all form part of the BIM. Non-graphic information is as significant in considering BIM as is graphic information, the two are inseparable. The same cataloguing, need for structure and quality control of contents is crucial if non-graphic information is to play its part. Indeed it could be argued that non-graphic information is more important, in that it usually contains the original design assumptions, briefing information, and the entire legal background to a job or the limitations of products given by manufacturers' specifications, for example.

Another dimension to non-graphic information is that it can also spill over quite significantly into the realms of office management and business strategy. The project BIM and especially the non-graphic information it contains could be used as the basis for office resourcing, future project resourcing, budgeting and future financial predictions. The graphic information usually finds its way into PR and marketing material and, especially these days, web sites. BIM becomes Business Information Modelling, or BBIM becomes Business and Building Information Modelling.

It's usually a struggle

In reality most attempts at BIM still include a multitude of systems strung together in a predominantly ad hoc way. The project team assemble themselves as contracts, client investment, budget expenditure, tender procedures and time scales develop. Project team members struggle as best they can or as their project commitment and individual business outlook dictate. From a purely quantitative standpoint the ability to apply metrics to assess what benefit has been achieved is illusive. Most built environment activity is unique and therefore it is difficult to establish a benchmark against which change can be measured.

There may be pockets of success. Reports on individual projects generally show fractured improvements. News from each project usually shows benefit in perhaps two or three selected areas. The time has not yet come when a BIM approach shows consistent and enduring change on all fronts. Benefits have been identified on some large scale projects, but they still portray a multitude of software platforms being used by design teams and supply chains to simply gain advantage in very specific areas, for example designing, co-ordinating and constructing a complex cladding system or detecting clashes between HVAC installations and structural elements. These benefits might be very worthwhile but they hardly reflect a revolution in managing information throughout project life cycle. Most

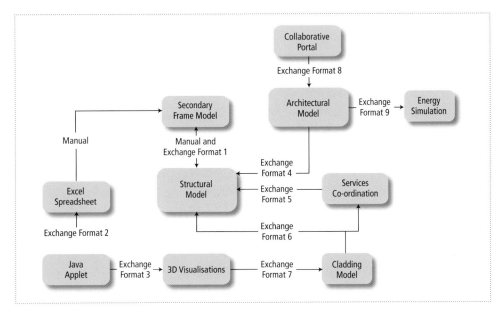

FIGURE 2.4 A cross section of software platforms and exchange formats taken from a recent project.

of what is reported is achieved with systems that are undergoing a natural evolution; there is no need or any special significance in calling this BIM.

BIM – a state of mind

Earlier, it was suggested that BIM is an emerging definition. If we look beneath the spin of BIM, BIM might be a manifestation of any combination of topics. In many respects it does not matter. BIM as a tangible entity does not exist. Despite optimism and vigorous marketing there is no distinct product that can be bought that is a BIM system. BIM is not an individual platform, nor a particular portal, group of people or type of information. BIM is not a single model or database. Even in a simple form on a very small scale, BIM will probably be two or more means of storing data; for example, a CAD system and a folder and file structure generated with Microsoft Office might be the BIM for a small architectural practice. Consistency of naming and categorising different types of information form the BIM in this context.

BIM is both an incomplete and infinite concept. It is incomplete in that it may consist of any combination of ingredients and infinite because there is no boundary to the scope of information that could be included in a project or have an effect on it, or impact elsewhere. A more appropriate interpretation of the BIM acronym might be 'Building Information

Management'. There would then be a better fit between the acronym and what is currently being discussed under the 'Modelling' banner. Discussions might be more productive if they considered whether BIM is a system or a group of systems; what business benefits there might be or what the business case for BIM actually is. It would eliminate the red herring debate of whether any software platform is a BIM or not. In this context any system is simply a tool to be used in managing information to the best of the ability of system functionality and its users.

PLIM (Project Lifecycle Information Management) is an even better acronym. It encompasses a cradle-to-grave idea for any project large or small. BIM as currently discussed has been stretched into the downstream phases of final construction and handover to facilities managers. By far the majority of discourse about BIM tacitly implies that it embodies design and construction. Little has been said about BIM in the earlier stages of development. It could and should include ideas of strategy, business case and design assumptions for large scale long term projects such as hospital or university development.

The Strategic Forum for Construction's Integration Project Toolkit may just as well be regarded as a manifestation of BIM in that it advocates integrated and non-adversarial working; it focuses on collaboration and the minimisation of duplication including information. If adopted, the SFC's toolkit would result in providing at least the same benefits and potentially more than the software vendors and their supermarket of software. Moreover, the SFC underpins its toolkit with a different form of contract and methods of procurement, something the software vendors do not engage with.

The JCT Constructing Excellence form of contract could also be construed as a form of BIM, in the sense that here is a legal instrument that offers a far more profound basis for working together to achieve benefits for the whole project team without necessarily recourse to technological solutions. BIM is a catalyst for change. Many of the benefits highlighted in surveys and research papers – such as it improves co-ordination; it reduces the number of Requests For Information; it reduces risk and certainly claims about improvements in design – could be achieved in any case. Even with disparate software platforms and platforms that do not claim to be BIM, all that is needed within the project team is a different way of thinking, a co-operative mindset.

In actual fact BIM is a state of mind, a set of principles. It is an outlook on how project information might be handled and in that sense is perhaps one of the most potentially potent factors to have emerged in recent times for better co-operative working; in one sense the sophistication of technology is an irrelevance. Culture change, a new state of mind, and shifts in perception cannot be forced by the use of technology, indeed technology can create more problems than it solves. When viewed objectively the current adversarial culture generating fractured and faulty information runs counter to the fact that what it produces has to be co-ordinated, harmonised and must perform as a cohesive whole. The trick is to get everyone in the office or project to enter the same state of mind. This begins to sound like a yoga session rather than a hard-nosed project team way of working, but until everyone adopts the same mantra then implementing BIM in any shape or form will be an uphill struggle. Parties to the project have to be willing to countenance new methods of working and communicating and documenting their work. A willingness to adapt to a BIM way of working is essential if a new way of doing business is to generate qualitative and quantitative benefits.

Technology has invented a form of information paralysis. Never has it been so easy to generate information and issue it to the public domain. Filtering what information is needed, deciding what can be used effectively and keeping it tidy are the difficult tasks. Newer forms of contract and agreements and guidance on standards and compatibilities between software will help enormously in supporting a shift in mind set, but the crucial ingredient is to want to adopt BIM for the benefit of you, your client and the project team. Hopefully different ways of working and new technological techniques do herald the beginning of a significant change in the way we work in architecture and construction. Once there is a realisation that better information husbandry leads to less litigation and improved surety of time scales, then innovative forms of contract and patterns of insurance cover not yet envisaged will follow. These are key issues if a genuine shift in culture and perceptions is to take place.

BIM is a state of mind that views:

- A different practice strategy.
- A new business opportunity accessed via the agreement with the client.
- A different fee and resource pattern across the *RIBA Plan of Work*.
- A positive legal landscape.
- A team committed to co-operation.
- A new combination of roles, responsibilities and processes.
- A reliance and basic understanding of object technology.

▶ **SUMMARY**

The who, what and when of applying BIM

- Decide who to involve – is it the immediate team or the widest possible community?

- Will BIM be implemented outside the conventional design and construction phases?

- Remember, any type of information can be included in a BIM approach.

- Relatively new forms of co-operative contract provide a better legal landscape.

- In the end BIM is what the team want it to be and is as successful as they want to make it.

SECTION 3
BIM ingredients

Many commentaries and case studies on the uses of BIM currently available, especially on the web, refer to techniques that have been around from the beginning of CAD. In many instances the technique is used in the same way it has been used for the past four decades. However, BIM represents a shift in perception of the way the technique has been adapted to better effect. The ingredients described in this section can be found to a greater or lesser extent and in any combination in any of the examples now being published as BIM working. They range from the most basic 2D drafting techniques to ideas of parametrics, intelligent objects, portals and the cloud.

The purists may disagree with the headings chosen but the intention is not to satisfy any highly technical analysis of BIM or an academic discourse about BIM, but to give mainstream practice some working concepts. This will allow them to calibrate themselves as to where they are, as well as their position in relation to others when it comes to managing information. In addition it should give some comfort that everyone is involved with BIM in actual fact; it is not the domain of technical wizards or large organisations. Every architectural practice can improve its BIM performance by identifying and understanding better the ingredients they already use, as well as forming targets for developing BIM further in an office or project context at their own pace and with their own individual priorities.

2D 'drawings'

The popular way of using early CAD systems was to simply use them as computerised drawing boards. Very few took the new invention to be a chance to manage computer drawn information in new and improved ways. Early techniques offered the opportunity to overlay information, for example one floor plan on top of another; this enables the co-ordination of structure and service cores from one floor to another. Standard office floors need only be drawn once and then variations made for basement, ground and roof levels.

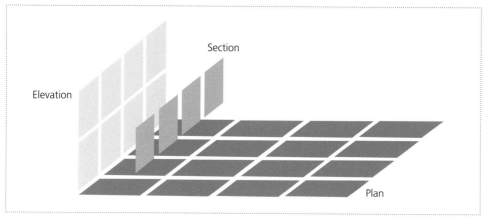

FIGURE 3.1 'Tablets' of graphics make up plan, section and elevation planes.

Major planes through the project are defined as a grid of individual graphics 'tablets'. Each tablet contains all the information for that particular part of the project and does not represent a 'drawing' on a piece of paper. For a large project any given plan, section or elevation plane may contain many tablets. Architectural, structural and HVAC information can be 'stacked' on each graphics tablet but carefully structured with the assistance of naming conventions. Updates and new contributions are made on a regularly agreed and quality controlled basis. This approach represents the first tentative steps any practice can take towards implementing BIM. At its simplest this method, especially in terms of graphic information, has at its heart the use of one widespread file format. The most popular is

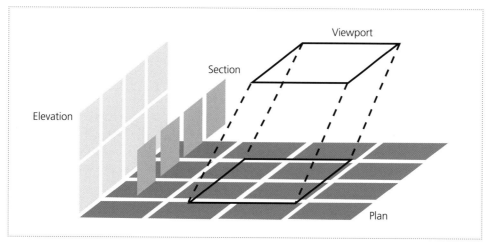

FIGURE 3.2 A viewport determines what information appears on a drawing sheet.

usually taken as .DWG drawing file format. Most CAD packages can export .DWG format files, so different software platforms could contribute to a central .DWG graphic database.

A viewport onto an area selects the combination and scale of information required at any time to produce a conventional paper drawing.

One software platform

There are several leading players in the field of architectural and construction software claiming that their offering is a complete BIM system, providing a very comprehensive repository for project information. A closer look at these platforms will probably reveal a central component or components that are the historical and technical evolution of their core CAD system. In addition there will probably be a considerable suite of other components that provide additional functionality, for example schedules, environmental evaluations, structural analysis, project programming and costings. To what extent BIM can be achieved by any single software platform depends on several key factors:

- Which of the major software platforms does each company in the project team possess and to what extent are they compatible?
- How many components within a particular software package does each project team member possess and use with strategic and practical competence?
- Do the project team players have compatible levels of expertise? This is perhaps one of the most important factors.
- The more components used within differing systems across several companies, the more difficult managing information will be.

The system vendor likes to extol the virtues of using component after component of their software and perhaps in their own right and in relatively isolated demonstration circumstances there may be advantage in their use. But when used with a myriad of other components from a range of systems in a project context over a protracted period of time, the story is very different.

Currently the big selling point for the single software platform method is that if a change is made somewhere in 'the model' then all appropriate information is updated at the same time. This is a double-edged sword. It may save a great deal of drudgery when amending information for any reason. Do not underestimate how much care must be taken that the new state of information held on the single software platform is still compatible, for example with performance specifications, reports to the client and legal and statutory requirements. There is still a checking process to be carried out to ensure that information is still valid within the single software platform and outside it, because, at the moment there is no single software platform that can handle the infinite and dynamic information types associated with building stock.

Objects

Object technology is a profound invention. It has revolutionised our lives. People are often surprised to find that they are likely to use object technology every day. It is what drives the web and all its facilities such as search, social media, information archiving and much more. It allows many systems, whether on mobile phones, desktop computers, 'clouds', wireless communications and GPS systems, to work together. The extent to which object technology percolates through our lives in the 21st century is immense.

We now think of the internal combustion engine's first appearances as quite rudimentary in comparison to a Formula 1 racing car's engine, or the engines in modern heavy transport, or military vehicles. However, we are only at Mr Ford's or Mr Karl Benz's stage of development.

What is an object?

In the software world an object is quite straightforward, it is simply 'an instance of a class'. The unsuspected simplicity of this expression belies its power in providing a different and exciting generation of software that represents a quantum change and will affect the way we work well into the future. Actually, class is the most significant word in the expression and means 'a collection of things that exhibit the same characteristics and behaviour'. Transferring these ideas into architecture and construction all components have:

* dimensions
* material
* description.

Universal behaviour that applies to all types of component is impossible to identify.

The next level of classification reveals other characteristics:

Type of Component	Specific Characteristics
Openings	Clear opening
Structure	Span, bending, shear
Ironmongery	Lock type
HVAC	Air flow rate

FIGURE 3.3 Typical component characteristics.

Put simply, an object is something that carries information and can do something. At the extremes it can carry nothing but information or nothing but the ability to do something. More typically an object will contain both information and action. Also it is unlikely that any real world entity would be represented by one object alone; it is more likely that a whole series of objects are involved to represent the characteristics and behaviour of even the simplest of components.

Consider how a word processor – such as the one used to write this book – controls the formatting of paragraphs. Each time I press 'enter' to make a new paragraph, I create a paragraph marker ('¶') which might be thought of as the object that contains information about the font, style and current justification of the paragraph. No matter how many times I reformat the document, shuffle or edit paragraphs, all the objects involved 'know' what information is involved and how they should behave to achieve my desired layout.

It is a good illustration of collections of objects working together – and a particularly instructive one too because it shows how many object technologies can control non-graphic information just as they can control graphical data – just as much of the information contained in the BIM environment is non-graphic too.

FIGURE 3.4 Everyday objects and behaviour.

The new design team member

Some types of information and behaviour can be identified for the world of architecture and construction, which determine the relationship one component might have with another. Relationships can be represented as objects. For example, one component may have to have an association with another; all ductwork passing through the enclosure to a protected stairway should be so fitted that all joints between the ductwork and the enclosure are fire stopped. Some components must not be associated with others, for example air transfer grilles should not be fitted in any door, wall, floor or ceiling enclosing a protected stairway otherwise there would be a path for fire to spread.

These associations will consist of information about the conditions of the relationship of one component relative to another as well as behaviour about preventing or allowing the association. When associations are defined then the next step is to enable these component objects to do something about the situation they find themselves in. They can be equipped to check their context and make suitable adjustments. In the first example above, if a piece of ductwork finds itself passing through a fire barrier, it could then introduce the necessary fire stopping automatically. The characteristics of the ductwork might be a list of all other components which represented a protected stairway. The behaviour would be for the ductwork to check what it found itself adjacent to or passing through. Similarly in the second case, a characteristic of the grille might be a list of all other components in which it should not be installed, and the behaviour would be software that checked what the grille was being fitted into.

Given the current and future sophistication of software and the increasing effort that is being spent on researching these ideas about objects in architecture and construction, then it is not difficult to envisage a day when objects will make decisions for themselves once they have been included in the BIM. Even if their contributions remain at the relatively detailed scale as the ones illustrated above, taken together the potential for them to alter the state of any design model is significant and they can be viewed as members of the design team in their own right.

Parametrics

Parametrics has just been discovered by some prestigious architectural practices, but the concept has been around since the beginning of CAD systems. The OXSYS/BDS/GDS system developed jointly by Oxford Regional Health Authority and Applied Research of Cambridge was making use of parametrics almost 40 years ago. Parametrics at its most basic in this context can be illustrated by simply supplying dimensions to a generic form; for example the basic formula for the volume of a cylinder is $\pi r^2 h$. Giving different values of 'r' and 'h' will produce different sizes and proportions of cylinder; in fact the range is infinite.

In a practical context the simple equation can represent the whole family of pipework no matter what the pipework is used for. Adding a simple piece of information such as its material characteristic will turn it into a copper water pipe, a plastic drainage pipe or a concrete stormwater pipe. Putting two of the equations together with differing 'r's would give us the material thickness, and so on. There is no limit to the amount of information that can be added to the basic generic form to enable it to represent any kind of pipework. The values for the simple parametric model can be obtained by either the user typing in values or by the user placing an elastic version which obtains its values from the positions the user 'hits' during placement. Taking the cylinder example above, the mouse would be used to indicate two different positions that could give the value of the radius. Similarly two positions could give the value of the height or length of the cylinder.

A slightly more sophisticated form of parametrics is the combination of the generic item and the idea that other objects can carry information about relationships and adjacency conditions. Imagine a straightforward vertical four storey facade that the designer wishes to clad with a proprietary cladding panel system. Given the elevation is displayed on a computer screen, the user may indicate the required positions and sizes of window openings. Then the user indicates the overall area where the cladding system is required. Objects can suggest an optimum panel layout depending on some external parameter such as minimum wastage or an optimum panel size for manual as opposed to mechanically assisted installation.

Intranets, extranets, portals and clouds

It is useful to have a simple working concept of intranets and extranets. The former is a network of computers and users within a company connected through the internet or with hard wires or a combination of both. An extranet is a network of computers and users connected via the internet that spreads to the world outside a company's boundaries extending its information and/or operation to a defined selection of other users.

The Shorter Oxford English Dictionary defines portal in a computing context as 'a website providing a directory of links to other sites and often a search engine and other facilities'. Alternatives in the dictionary convey ideas of gateways being stately or elaborate. Both shades of meaning shed light on what is available. The computing version is obvious but portals do involve a certain amount of ceremony both in their creation and operation; they appear foreboding, intricate and complicated to many people.

At a very general level, commercially available portals converge on the idea of a place, a virtual space where access by many can be obtained to information and a multitude of services and techniques for managing information. There are several leading portal products available to architectural and construction project teams, some with application in a wider project life cycle context where information is a long term asset for large property portfolios.

The basics

At one end of the spectrum all portals offer some form of document management, a simple information repository for as many members of the project team who wish to participate. Graphic and non-graphic information of any kind can be sent to the portal. In a document management role, the portal assists any project team to keep track of who donated information; what type it is; what status it has in terms of being provisional or final; how many revisions it has undergone and who it is issued to; the list is endless. Usually the opportunity is offered for the team to add any other information attribute that it believes necessary for the good of the project. Some portals allow comments or red marking to be added to documents, both graphic and non-graphic; perhaps indicating where information is unco-ordinated and extra clarification is required.

Often the portal has its own cataloguing and indexing system. Portals will manage details about all members of the project team, their practice status, roles and responsibilities and especially their e-mail addresses which will probably be used for automatic alerts for timely reminders about the issue and receipt of information.

Building queries and searching for various groups of information is a basic function of the information portal as it becomes more and more populated. The project team usually have to agree among themselves how the information is to be stored but once that is achieved a variety of reports can be extracted. Information portals usually offer an audit trail facility covering the complete history of all transactions. This storehouse of information packages forms the fundamental background to an abundance of other types of functionality that address different aspects of information management and team collaboration. This allows what in the past was done 'by hand' to be done in a more efficient, structured way.

What else do portals offer?

Workflow modelling and calendar functionality for programming key dates or reminders about the timing of information issues are common features. The ability to request information and give responses provides the team with a discussion forum for construction problems. Analysis on this type of activity forms a major part of the reporting function of the portal. Monitoring reports can then support incentives for progress or in less fortunate circumstances bases for claims and litigation.

The most up-to-date portals at the time of writing begin to offer more sophisticated project management techniques. For example, risk reports can be aggregated into a central risk register and, linked to other applications, can give commentaries on how risk management is progressing. A second example of the latest thinking and with wider implication is to begin to incorporate forms of contract into the portal or other software functionality. Previous sections have given working concepts of objects, their behaviours, information content and ability to encapsulate relationships. There is no reason why these ideas should not be extended to contracts and insurance policies which could 'behave', carry information and detect relationships with other forms of software application to provide commentary on legal obligations and contractual matters.

Problems with portals

A fundamental issue with proprietary portals is that as information warehouses they are good at monitoring packages of information but offer no help in terms of prescribing how their contents should be structured. Imagine a warehouse full of different size boxes. The warehouse manager accepts boxes from various deliveries; he can see inside each box and therefore knows what it contains. He has a system for deciding where to keep the boxes and who else can look inside. He can also write messages to other people on the outside and he knows who to pass the box onto and when. What he cannot do is decide how the contents are arranged, nor does he have any power over those who delivered the boxes to tell them how the contents should be arranged.

Portals are another expensive overhead. They must earn their keep so the return on investment calculation must confirm that the purchase and ongoing costs provide some benefit in terms of better co-ordinated information, advantage from collaboration or fewer claims. The first two are relatively difficult to quantify and so an investment in portal participation is something of a leap in the dark. Portals also incur overhead in terms of attitude from those using it. Very often scepticism about usefulness is a barrier to achieving financial or any other benefit. Any practice usually contains its own particular mix of champions and sceptics. It is not always easy to match priorities across projects with the availability of individuals who are willing to try something new and positive.

Team members have to be trained, but training is always a low financial priority in many practices. All too often, increases in bottom line performance are expected from the use of any form of IT within a company without properly providing the expertise to do so. Portals can be prone to simply mimicking current bad practice and compartmentalisation of information and endeavour. Project team members sometimes insist that they have their own area on the portal and allow nobody else access or restricted access. This obviously defeats the whole object of using the portal in the first place. Even though a portal is being used there is no guarantee that the perceived or marketed benefits will be realised.

Some vendors offer templates for the way projects could be organised. This may be a starting point but every representative of every practice coming to the 'portal table' will have their own idea of how things should be organised, usually along the lines of how they themselves do it. Unless preordained in advance either by a consultant backed by a powerful player in the team or by some tight contractual specification on portal use the time taken to reconcile diverse thinking should not be underestimated.

For some time now we have faced the problem of different CAD systems in use on a project and the problems that it brings in terms of organising and co-ordinating information. Large practices got around the CAD problem by having more than one CAD system in their office. Now we have another layer superimposed on that, the proliferation of portals. Powerful and large team players can contractually dictate which portal to use and could perhaps afford to support more than one. However, most practices in architecture and construction are classified as small companies and would struggle to support the operation of more than one portal.

Clouds

A curious phenomenon has emerged in recent years whereby we use less of our own personal computer whether desktop or laptop and more of someone else's computing power out on the web. That is not to say that our own computer power is not used; it is, but we have moved from a position where we used our own computer exclusively in our own domestic or work environment to a position where servers supporting the internet do a large proportion of searching and computing for us.

Some want the internet to become the universal computing machine where the entire web network becomes as fast to each individual user as their own laptop or desktop. It certainly is quick already, but given that the majority of the world's population want to use the web more and more, the speed and capacity of the web needs to be increased to monumental proportions. This may happen. It is worth delving a little deeper into the concept so that reasonable extrapolations can be inferred for BIM. The cloud is in fact very much down to earth in that it is simply millions of servers located in the premises of companies that support web services. Originally these companies simply used their servers to carry out their web hosting business, but eventually realised that there was a market to sell server space to large businesses who did not want to carry the overhead of managing their own servers.

Cloud computing is being exploited by very large companies where the staffing, security accommodation and some communications costs are a major overhead component. In effect they are buying in a large chunk of computing power which is managed on their behalf by a third party at a remote location.

IaaS – Infrastructure as a Service

Currently, buying the most basic level of a cloud facility, namely server space, networking, data storage and probably the ability to run several operating systems such as Solaris, Linux and Windows, has limited attraction for any project team. This package means the user can and has to build their own database and software applications on top of the infrastructure. A project team is unlikely at the moment to shoulder the overhead of building anything on top of this. It is true that software platforms and database systems could be installed on a

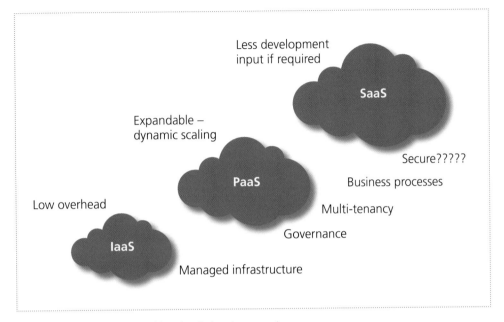

Less development
input if required

SaaS

Expandable –
dynamic scaling

Secure?????

PaaS

Business processes

Low overhead

Multi-tenancy

Governance

IaaS

Managed infrastructure

FIGURE 3.5 Three notional levels of cloud computing.

common cloud platform but overall there would be little or no advantage over the familiar struggle with disparate CAD/BIM systems and collaborative portals.

Amazon's Elastic Compute Cloud is one of the leading examples of an IaaS. Amazon built its online shop, but found it had spare capacity so it began to sell the basic tools for others to build their own applications. Today the Amazon portal is not only a window onto the Amazon shop itself but is the 'mall' if you like where others have built their own virtual shops which operate in their own way.

PaaS – Platform as a Service

This includes IaaS but in addition there is what is known as a development environment. The cloud customer is given software tools to write their own applications within a particular context. For example, Google's App Engine enables applications to be built and hosted using the same systems that power Google applications. This means that a practice could build their own customisations for using Google Docs, Google Calendar and GMail for instance, as some form of project management, risk management or communal specification system.

SaaS – Software as a Service (also known as 'On-demand Software')

All the above are included, but SaaS is aimed at a particular business function or functions. The SaaS environment must be attractive enough to many customers with similar requirements. For example, the cost of writing and maintaining accounting software is very expensive for large companies, so the SaaS vendor provides a generalised accounting package that each individual cloud customer can use.

This has been just a short and relatively superficial skirmish into the world of cloud computing. The general benefits are meant to be:

- Scalability and/or elasticity of supply and demand.
- A managed but outsourced IT capability.
- Reduced capital and revenue expenditures.
- Faster development and/or deployment of software applications.
- Better business agility.

This is a significant and fast growing industry. There are many variations offered and the distinctions between IaaS, PaaS and SaaS become blurred. Nevertheless, there is a significant trend developing which will inevitably impact on architecture and construction.

It may be some time before mainstream practice sees advantage in such facilities. Costs and ease of use have to meet before the prospect looks attractive for relatively small businesses in architecture and construction. But it probably will happen that practices buy their computing power from the web rather like buying electricity or gas from a provider.

Standards

No examination of BIM would be complete without considering information standards, after all it is the 'Information' in BIM that is the most powerful factor. The topic of standards is wide but unfortunately it is not given the prominence it deserves. Adopting standards leads to creating, using and maintaining information in a far more effective way – and is a necessary platform for BIM. Once again we find that a powerful tool for managing information is available at little investment cost. What's stopping you?

What is meant by standards in this context? A simple working concept is to think of any personal or business computer, laptop or desktop, it makes no difference. There are two overall structuring concepts that tell the story of how information is managed at this level: files and folders. Everyone is familiar with folders and files, but they are not used to their full potential as a powerful means of structuring information. Given some basic conventions they can provide an extremely useful means of structuring information.

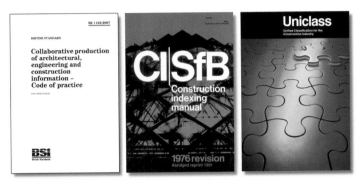

FIGURE 3.6 Industry information standards.

BS 1192 (2007)

BS 1192 (2007) is the latest in a long line of British Standards that have tried to help the production of information in an architectural world. From the earliest days of simple drawing board procedures to today's world of sophisticated object technology this standard has evolved to give professionals a helping hand on how they can manage the information that passes through their hands or computers on a daily basis.

The standard has been developed with the use of public money through the British Standards Institution. What remains a mystery is that most companies in architecture and construction spend significant sums and a great deal of time in some cases making a case for why this standard does not meet their needs and so develop one of their own. The standard gives guidance on how to produce a communal pool of information and shows how information can flow through a private working area, a shared public repository, an issued area and onto being archived. Additional codes can be attached to information to give further clarity on its reliability status.

CI/SfB

The CI/SfB Construction Indexing Manual first published in 1962 provides a means of classifying and structuring information in the BIM environment. It was specifically devised to provide a structure for project information and is as relevant today as it was back in the sixties.

The standard consists of five tables that cover:

Table 0	**Physical Environment**	Wide range of building typologies
Table 1	**Elements**	Standard classification of building elements
Table 2	**Construction Forms**	Classifies main construction forms
Table 3	**Materials**	Classifies materials that form a product
Table 4	**Activities, requirements**	Functional activities and product characteristics

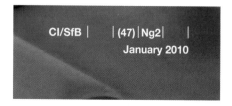

FIGURE 3.7 An example of a CI/SfB classification.

Almost every product catalogue or piece of literature discreetly carries a portion of this classification system. When requesting product information from the web you will spot that the cover page of the .pdf has the distinctive combination of characters which tells the story of what it is. This is a very succinct language for classifying information that can be used directly in software platforms for naming layers, levels or object libraries for example.

The figure above shows part of the front cover of the .pdf download for clay interlocking tiles from Marley Eternit Interlocking roof systems:

- (47) is from Table 1, the elemental classification, telling us it is a 'Roof finish'
- 'N' is from Table 2, telling us it is 'Rigid sheet overlap work'
- 'g2' is from Table 3, telling us it is 'Fired clay, vitrified clay or ceramics'.

UNICLASS

UNICLASS or Unified Classification for the Construction Industry is a similar system. It was first published in 1997 and is based on ISO TR 14177. It has fifteen tables giving a wider classification range, covering for example forms of information, spaces, construction elements, work sections and more besides:

A	Form of Information	J	Work Sections for Buildings
B	Subject Disciplines	K	Work Section for Civil Engineering Works
C	Management	L	Construction Products
D	Facilities	M	Construction Aids
E	Construction Entities	N	Properties and Characteristics
F	Spaces	P	Materials
G	Elements for Buildings	Q	Universal Decimal Classification
H	Elements for Civil Engineering Works		

FIGURE 3.8: UNICLASS tables for classifying information

The following extract from the UNICLASS document gives an insight into what is covered by the system, but it and the table above belie the incredibly comprehensive tool this classification system provides for managing information. 'UNICLASS is a classification scheme for organising library materials and for structuring product literature and project information. It incorporates both CAWS (Common Arrangement of Works Sections for Building Works) and EPIC (Electronic Product Information Co-operation), a new system for structuring product data and product literature.'

Mix your own ingredients

There is far more to be said about the subtleties and application of any of these ingredients, but it is the choice of each individual practice and project team how they align themselves using these topics as a broad checklist and strategy for more co-operative and effective ways of using information.

As with any good recipe it is important to choose the correct combination and quality of ingredients if the recipe is to satisfy. An analysis of how these ingredients are used and could be used and then combined with some of the new forms of co-operative contract mentioned later can make orders of magnitude of difference to profitability, office and project team culture and most of all to the quality of what is built.

► **SUMMARY**

BIM ingredients

• There are many ingredients that can be used in what is now called a BIM environment.

• 2D/3D graphic databases are a good and workable form of BIM without necessarily investing in expensive software.

• Compiling an object library on any software platform requires a degree of pre-preparation and therefore investment up front.

• Portals can be a help if planned into the workflow properly otherwise they will be yet another issue that brings disillusionment.

• Parametrics are useful for relatively sophisticated 3D co-ordination work.

• Classification standards are well developed and can be adopted for little effort but great benefit.

SECTION 4
The business case for BIM

A business case signifies a dedication to improving practice performance. Various drivers are quoted, and the benefits, risks and measurable outcomes should be clearly identified. Usually the main underlying impetus is towards improved profitability.

There are many business drivers attributed to BIM:

- Return on investment and increased profitability.
- Increased efficiency, a reduction in alterations and RFIs.
- Amorphous areas such as better design, confidence in design, design functionality.
- More sustainable outcomes to built environment interventions.
- Benefits due to substantive practice restructuring.
- Greater collaboration in terms of improved information management, clearer communications and revised workflows that reflect better integration of team activity.
- Increased opportunities for offering additional value-added services that the company would not normally contemplate.
- More accurate project cost estimates.
- Improved timescales.
- Co-ordinated visualisations to help construction proceed or help clients appreciate how the project is developing.
- Automatic detailing and scheduling take off.

These drivers are quoted over and over again in reviews, worked examples and web site propaganda. They are universal drivers for almost any strategy for improvement for any company in architecture and construction.

It is not a case of what can BIM do for you, but what can you do with BIM to achieve progress.

Conventional rule of thumb wisdom suggests a three-year cycle for financial and other potential successes to appear in any business. The first year is anticipated to be a loss, the second year breaks even and the third year shows a profit.

For example, if there were an intention to open a branch office there would be an immediate overhead in finding and setting up new premises, finding the right staff and ensuring all necessary insurances were in place, as well as spending money on publicising the new event. Even if work was ready and waiting at the new location there would be initial expense in finding working capital until fees began to flow. It is important to realise that the same wisdom needs to be applied to BIM. Instant results should not be expected.

Whose business case?

Each of the business case drivers will cross the boundaries of clients, consultant disciplines, constructors, supply chains, operators and users. They all have a vested interest in seeking improvement either tangible or intangible under the business driver headings. Each can implement a BIM strategy in their own right, but as things stand it would naturally be their own practice's business interests that would be put first. The magic moment is to get as many of these players as possible to make their own business interests coincide with those of the project and each other.

A coherent business case relies on a clear statement of objectives and outcomes, the clearer the better. Businesses are likely to have their own agendas which may include more than one interrelated business case, offering the possibility of better performance all round. Changes in culture are a collective initiative, and it takes time for there to be a realisation that every interest should coincide.

The nature of architecture and construction makes it difficult to invent a system of metrics that will clearly and simply evaluate how one project has generated benefit, financial or otherwise, over another. Projects are unique in the main; architects create prototypes, and there is little opportunity to repeat a design. The likelihood of the next prototype working depends on the accumulation of collective expertise over time rather than having the ability to refine a design model until a production run is put in place.

Tracking benefit can be a tricky process – many variables and distinctive aspects of every project make it a severe challenge to compare a project that used BIM with a similar project that did not. What to measure is perplexing. If measurements are made on a financial basis alone then a return on investment would be difficult to evaluate. This outlook would concentrate on the financial considerations of gauging whether benefit had accrued or not. There would be a whole series of analyses and monitoring processes to establish what the investment input had been in order to measure the return.

Can we afford it?

Or: Can we afford not to? The question of scale rears its head again. At one level for the small or medium sized office there may be little to afford. Good information management need not imply great expenditure. Modest cost could arise simply by instigating a review of company processes and information management. Changing to different ways of doing things would involve some disruption costs but if carefully planned need not stretch the bank too far. For larger offices moving to BIM might require expenditure which would have to be part of normal budgeting procedure. More education/training, change management, hardware and software requirements and recruitment will all require customary treatment.

Can we afford not to in a changing market? Whatever the BIM benefits, the controversy is now out there, the hare is running. Clients are increasingly catching on to BIM, and while some will see it as a means of attempting to drive fees and prices down, the enlightened will want a better quality outcome. Whichever it is the market will absorb the new BIM phenomenon and operate on a different dynamic in the future. Affording BIM plays its part in the constant quest for improvement. Architects are not only seeking to provide better solutions in the built environment but also continually searching for better ways of doing so. There are commercially better ways and for those with the inclination, BIM is a means of improving office working and job satisfaction.

What effect will it have on salary levels?

Have we got the appropriate staff and are we happy with what we pay them for what becomes their specialist expertise? Some recruitment now focuses on specialist job titles for BIM, ranging from BIM Director to BIM Junior Technician. In many examples job advertisements simply substitute BIM for CAD. However some recruitment drives do give the impression of trying to embark on something new. Job adverts are asking for people with a wide skill set, ranging across a responsibility for creating and executing an implementation plan for developing clients to having Building Information Management capabilities in their entirety. This would include the development of processes, policies and procedures; an in-depth knowledge of building processes; several years' experience in construction and previous experience of leading and managing BIM teams. Serious attempts are being made to find high calibre people capable of taking a business in a different strategic direction.

The BIM Manager title covers many possibilities, ranging through the management of CAD in a large multi-location office, developing the company's BIM processes and policies and as a consequence advising on business change. A BIM Co-ordinator supervises an individual project BIM or BIMs, while a '3D Junior CAD Technician (BIM)' can expect to be modelling in 3D. Whatever the state of play now, BIM in any manifestation is a trend that is here to stay and there will be a certain amount of spin on the part of employment agencies, potential employers and employees in what is said to generate mutual attraction.

However, as the more serious players emerge on both sides of the fence then it is likely that those who can demonstrate successful BIM implementations will command a salary premium and that companies who feel BIM has obtained commercial advantage for them will want to retain the staff who created it. The use of BIM might mean a move from using fewer contract staff and more permanent staff. There could be a realisation that BIM is more to do with information management and information integration as well as a combination of business process and strategy; it is more than knowing the exigencies and idiosyncrasies of CAD. If so, then the people with this newer strain of expertise will be the custodians of a longer term business asset and opportunity. The balance might change between contract rates, agency fees and disruption costs as against higher permanent salaries to ensure continuity in a growing key area. Just how much this manifests itself is open to speculation. The metrics for identifying salary increase directly related to BIM are as elusive as those measuring BIM advantage itself.

How much do we invest in training?

Have we got the appropriate training at all levels? Do we need more? The straightforward and simple answer to this question is: as much as you can possibly afford and on a continuing basis. Training is a critical but underestimated investment. There is a rule of thumb about software that says if you spend 'x' on software, you will need to budget for '10x' on training, and '100x' and upwards on information. This approximation is difficult to translate into today's world of site licences, enterprise licences, subscription licensing and so on, but it still rings true and illustrates the notion that expenditure on software is relatively minimal. The real spending begins afterwards.

BIM implies a change in methods, anything from being consistent about where origins are placed in CAD files to entirely different business procedures. New expertise has to be developed step by step alongside existing knowledge so that the office and ongoing projects are not jeopardised. Training plans for BIM should be seen as an integral part of the strategy for developing the office and not as a piecemeal, sporadic activity that fills in quiet gaps in workload. Usually a core of enthusiasts will plan and implement a training programme for other members of the company. What their plan entails depends on which aspects of BIM are already in place and which others are seen as providing benefit.

Adequate time should be budgeted for trainees to acclimatise themselves to new ways of working and if necessary the business imperatives underlying what they are doing should be reiterated by senior members of staff.

Expenditure is rather analogous to the concepts of patent and latent defects. There is the obvious (patent) purchase of a training programme from the software vendor. Latent training happens by culture, being handed down from employee to employee, in which case there is a hidden cost when the trainer takes time to explain to the trainee, or where there is an absence of any form of training, which leads to problems and inefficiencies which have cost implications in themselves. However, training brings with it connotations of buying courses from a software vendor. A wider notion of education might be a more useful investment. The partner/director/CAD user divide has already been discussed but it is the fusion of existing and new knowledge gained by education that will transform the skills and abilities at all levels in a business into a new and powerful force using BIM.

Training bought from a vendor will do little if anything to show how any particular system mechanism plays its part in business case and business strategy. A very simple example is while there has been much effort spent on discussing standards for layers or levels there has to the author's knowledge never been an explicit discussion or guidance on how these devices fit into commercial strategy, legal obligations or operational efficiency. Every user has been left to formulate an opinion on what these mechanisms could do. Education about what these concepts are and how they play a key part in information management is required to be able to harness them properly.

Information management again is the key to how much to spend. The necessary knowledge may not be found in the obvious place, there are many worthwhile courses available on the web, at business schools and many other places outside architecture and construction.

Training in information management

Investment in training for BIM is popularly perceived as purchasing more courses from the 3D CAD vendor. Training courses of this kind do have a part to play, but it might be more pertinent to invest in information management training. Architects, indeed the whole project life cycle team, deal in information. It was always the case but the past decade has seen exponential growth in our capability to generate and maintain information.

Information has not only increased in quantity but also in complexity. Some estimates show as much as 80 per cent of vital business information is currently stored in unmanaged repositories, making its efficient and effective use a near impossibility. The content of many DWG/DGN files, other non-graphic files and Windows folder names in architectural and construction companies up and down the country no doubt corroborate that proposition. Proper information management enables businesses small or large to punch above their weight in terms of the size of project they can contemplate, be more competitive and better able to maintain growth and agility.

Information in architecture and construction is generated at many different points, making it difficult to ensure accuracy, consistency and completeness. The importance of information management does not figure to any great extent in the education of architects so it comes as no surprise that they neither grasp its significance nor are very good at it. The first reaction is usually to recruit architects for their design skills, not for their information management abilities. BIM may play a part in emphasising that it is not the software but information management that primarily requires investment. As the use of BIM increases and widens in application, information husbandry will drive project team players together, as will be needed to make BIM effective.

Alongside training in information management, technical training for specific aspects of BIM is important too. Parametric modelling, visualisations, formulating schedules and specialist consultant areas such as M&E or structures are all examples where conceptual and detailed expertise is required.

▶ SUMMARY

The business case for BIM

- The drivers for the BIM business case are no different from the drivers for any other kind of business improvement.

- Investment in BIM should be treated like any other long term business investment and not be expected to supply a profit revolution on one job.

- Training is not just for Christmas.

- Spend as much as possible on training.

- Senior people are probably the ones most in need of training.

- Training in information management might be better than purchasing training from the CAD vendor.

- Training should bridge the business/technology divide.

- Be prepared to pay a salary premium for those who create and maintain a valuable information asset.

- Information management in architecture and construction will play an ever increasing part in generating profit and reducing exposure to litigation.

SECTION 5
BIM in the office

BIM is for office and project; it provides an integrated management capability in both cases.

A question of scale

Considering scale as an aspect of BIM implementation has received little attention. Vested interests on behalf of software vendors and large scale project teams have defined an aura of BIM around larger scale projects and multi-disciplinary international practices. Software vendors and architectural and construction companies who can afford spin machines tend to congregate together in the belief that they represent all scales and types of operation.

Information about BIM and its use is rather like being in an information cocoon. The average size UK practice taking an interest in published BIM material will notice a bias towards large scale practice companies and case studies. However, BIM as a state of mind, a set of principles or a methodology is equally applicable to any scale of office from the one man band to the large scale, international multi-disciplinary practice.

The small scale office

In an office where there are perhaps simply a handful of people, even a project as modest as a household extension can conform to the tenets of BIM just as well, if not better perhaps, than the multi-million/billion pound prestigious project. Small offices might benefit from simply adopting a humble 2D approach to BIM within their own sphere of operation and may well be more cost effective than larger practices trying to be all things to all people.

Alterations, extensions and one-off new domestic properties, however prestigious, will involve accumulating a body of information on one occasion only. Nevertheless a BIM approach brings improvements through a cataloguing and record keeping structure, possibly not involving anything more than a simple 2D CAD system and Microsoft Office to cover word processing and spreadsheets. In this context interpreting BIM as a comprehensive and co-ordinated information entity would not only provide the obvious basis for recording job drawings, specifications, approvals, correspondence and so on, but also the basis for office management functions such as pricing future jobs, VAT and tax returns, PI insurance applications, other accountancy information and PR and marketing material.

If managed carefully at this scale, information gathered, structured and input once to the appropriate place could be 'sliced' many times in different ways to support a whole manner of office functions. In many respects, BIM for the individual architect is no more than a very consistent document management system, a system that includes both project drawings and other information together with general office management. BIM at this scale would readily become embedded in the way the business operated. The culture thus established would be a natural part of the induction process, if and when any staff turnover occurred.

Developed at this level BIM might provide several ways forward. At one level BIM would provide a means of achieving a continuous internal efficiency plan. Looking outside the office a well-developed BIM approach could form a useful basis for working with other like-minded people or for effectively fitting into a framework with larger players.

The medium scale office

A medium scale office might be a practice housed in one set of premises, or perhaps at two or three other geographical locations. All the benefits which accrue to the architect operating as an individual apply at this scale of practice. BIM provides the additional advantage of consistency when implemented internally within geographically separate offices. Job statistics and inter-office resourcing can be managed with greater accuracy.

At the present time it is more efficient and friendlier to the environment if we move around information rather than people to eradicate peaks in workload as a consequence of demanding clients. So to be able to kill two birds with one stone is an advantage in the sense that an over-stretched office might move information to a 'quieter' branch office in economically stringent times. To achieve this, it is crucial that information practice adheres to common conventions. Servers can be linked or remote access software can give one terminal the ability to 'see' another one and operate it remotely. It is relatively easy to connect offices together so that information standards can be communally developed, agreed, implemented and supervised. This can be achieved either by software that allows remote control of terminals, or by the connectivity through the CAD software platform or a collaborative portal, or by the purchasing of a level of cloud computing.

It is important that conventions are kept under constant review. If there are several offices then it is a good idea to form a small group of representatives from each office to monitor and modify conventions and standards when necessary. It is crucial to avoid ad hoc changes or additions to information standards, otherwise the benefits of the approach can be quickly dissipated. Managers of the office(s) should ensure that proper change control processes, albeit simple at this scale of operation, are in place.

Changes to standards may arise as a consequence of an appointment with a different client, working on a new and unfamiliar building type or embracing a new service to address a different market. Whatever the cause of the change, enhancements to standards should be managed strategically and tactically just the same as any other business activity.

The large scale office

Implementing BIM across multinational, multi-disciplinary practices can ensure consistency of information quality as it does for the smaller scale office. This is particularly useful when operating across countries of varying professional standards and where the criterion for information quality might not be so rigorous. A brand of expertise and a level of quality control can be exported anywhere in the world.

Multi-disciplinary businesses can go even further by using BIM as a means of integrating information from the different branches of expertise they embrace. Either fees can be reduced in competitive circumstances or profit levels enhanced in more favourable bidding climates. Either way the multi-disciplinary business should gain fiscal and qualitative advantage due to operating BIM. In the subsequent discussions about BIM it is important to keep the scale factor in mind; the characteristics of BIM may differ for different sizes of practice and the type of service offered but appropriate BIM principles are a benefit to all.

Office methodology – how do we change our working practices?

Changing working practices starts at the top; it is the partner/director level in any private or public practice that needs to take responsibility. BIM needs to be viewed as a business investment in the same way that expansion, new markets or opening another office might be. The first step must be to reach a common understanding of what BIM means in any given context. A far greater mutual understanding of business and technology at all levels within a practice will inevitably be required. This must be found and understood free of sales spin and overenthusiastic evangelism. Preceding sections of this book have illustrated the scope of technology, information and human resource that might be included in a BIM approach. Future sections will give practical advice on implementing BIM within the project office.

The next step must be to decide whether BIM is to be an internal management technique, a methodology to be used on a project irrespective of what others do, or an approach whose virtues and adoption are extolled to the wider project team and supply chains. There is an obvious and common sense progression here, but so often it is not translated into a rational longer term strategy. At this stage there is a compound decision to be made as to which ingredients of BIM are to be adopted and the extent to which it is to be implemented within and beyond the office.

Office – the partner/director/CAD user divide

Since CAD/BIM existed it has been the domain of 'techies'. This has to change. Historically systems got off to a bad start. A divide emerged because a younger generation, not business owners or managers, adapted to technology quicker. An older generation of manager/partner did not, either because it was totally alien to their age group, or through fear, or through an unwillingness to be seen asking advice and tuition from those 'beneath' them in the business.

Those responsible for making strategic decisions in architecture and construction businesses must acknowledge the fact that they need to get themselves into a position where they are conversant with some of the concepts involved in BIM. Alternatively they must forge a working relationship with a technologist who can be relied upon to understand more than just the technology.

The traditional CAD manager role is defunct. Integrated practice is the way to deliver BIM, and concentrating on CAD platforms will lead to less than optimum results. Integrated practice, including BIM, is a core business activity.

▶ SUMMARY

BIM in the office

- Remember BIM can embrace any type of information.

- BIM is applicable to any scale of office.

- Small offices can adapt to BIM quickly and are possibly capable of realising benefit quicker than larger practices.

- The technology used to create a BIM can be minimal – a 2D CAD system and Microsoft Office could be very effective.

- BIM can assist the quality control of design and construction information across several geographically separate locations.

- BIM can be a catalyst for integration in multinational, multi-disciplinary practice.

SECTION 6
BIM within the project

BIM within a project can be an agent for cohesion and collaboration. Collaboration can have almost opposite meanings. *The Oxford English Dictionary* gives its meaning as 'work jointly with' or 'co-operate traitorously with an enemy'. While the latter is a little extreme it does contain a mixture of elements often found in project teams. There are champions of BIM and the sceptics, whose outlook injects resistance at best and can introduce serious information quality problems at worst. Their input needs to be managed carefully.

Technology or methodology?

BIM viewed as technology is a delivery tool, BIM viewed as information management is a delivery methodology. In the former case the team must decide which software platforms are to be used and how information connections are to be made. Team members can learn a great deal about how different software platforms interact to form an information composite. It is essentially a technical problem. In the latter case the team are faced with a much wider ranging series of issues which will impinge on and probably change their individual ways of working in a profound way if BIM is to be used in any significant form. The client, the architect or the contractor are the players most likely to assemble the team and therefore play a major role in the BIM approach to be adopted. Sometimes the team will be brought together on pre-experience of companies who want to work in a different way, other times the team could be gathered together without any prior knowledge of working relationships.

Step 1	Bring the team together
Step 2	Agree on a BIM leader
Step 3	Agree to what extent BIM will have an influence
Step 4	Agree which ingredients of BIM should be used
Step 5	Write and sign up to a BIM agreement

One or more of these players should provide BIM leadership. There has to be a commitment to BIM which will be hard to engender in the first instance and even more difficult to sustain, especially on longer term projects and as other supporting groups join the BIM context. BIM can be a catalyst for change on a single project basis. Individuals or practices may be encouraged to abandon traditional processes and exchange them for a more collective approach. Entrenched and cherished working methods can be challenged; better information channels can be presented as a means of enhancing performance.

The team must decide as soon as possible to what extent they want BIM to have an influence and which components of BIM should be used to bring that about. A previous section highlighted the need to decide how far BIM is to reach within the team. The core team can be expected to have major responsibilities throughout the design and construction phases. Key supporting supply chain members and other specialist consultants are likely to perform discrete functions at specific times.

▶ SUMMARY
BIM within the project
• Technology and methodology must form an integrated whole for BIM to be successful.
• A BIM approach should be formulated as early as possible by those who assemble the project team.
• BIM needs more than one champion in the project team.
• The selection of like-minded people and the extent to which BIM will apply are key decisions which must be taken early.

SECTION 7
What new business opportunities come with BIM?

Promoting technology has never been a winning strategy; it is what can be achieved by using it effectively that matters.

BIM as an investment

Any mainstream practice can harness the potential commercial benefits of BIM given the will to do so. If a business case has been made for BIM and it becomes part of the commercial way of life in the office then investment in some simple techniques will pay dividends in the long run.

This straightforward build up of expertise can be done with little outlay. BS 1192 (2007), CI/SfB Elemental Classification Guide and UNICLASS can all be purchased for a relatively modest price. A small investment in any of these documents would release a many-times-fold benefit in the way the office manages its information. Using these guides not only provides a *modus operandi* but also has serious effects for the use of information as an asset on a project. So often early concept design drawings are discarded or ignored once their initial functions of winning the job and obtaining planning permission are complete. To some extent the same applies to general arrangement drawings and construction details. Using a BIM approach and guided by the BS and say CI/SfB, information can be structured at an early stage so that additions can be made to a 'base layer' (not an AutoCAD layer) and gradually more detail added. Use of the conventions in the documents would enable information in all of the mainstream software platforms to be selected and filtered at will, without having to do separate sets of drawings for individual scales or functions.

Do we charge extra fees?

The decision to charge extra fees depends on whether the practice wants to make its BIM expertise available to the outside world. Some clients will not know about BIM; there is no point in spoiling their view of life. If this is the case then the business can offer the client some other form of advantage or retain any financial benefit for itself. Of course the opportunity should be taken to charge the highest fee the client/market will stand. It depends when the practice wants to put BIM expertise in the shop window whether to charge for it or not.

As expertise builds then more work can be done reliably in less time or projects bigger than would otherwise have been contemplated can be chased. The business might want to keep this new efficiency to itself too, so that the bottom line is improved. The decision to market a BIM service should be considered carefully. The ARB Code of Conduct places an obligation upon architects not to promote services beyond their expertise. (See next page 'Beware the Code of Conduct'.) If an informed client requires comfort that a BIM service is available, then all the careful business planning and growth of BIM techniques that have occurred and been documented in the office will be proof that services are being offered with the proper level of expertise.

There is of course a risk that offering what to all intents and purposes is a more efficient service will almost certainly lead the client to asking for a reduction in fee. If the body of information produced on a project has value to the client as an information asset, then there is added value which should be paid for, otherwise it is a question of negotiating skills.

Add more value using forms of appointment

The traditional services offered in the RIBA's forms of architects' appointment are obvious candidates for adding value. Information and co-ordination adds value and benefits which should be grounds for charging extra fees. Many factors quoted as part of the business case for using BIM are drivers for better business in any case, no matter what innovation is planned. The same is true when looking for value-added service within the forms of appointment.

For example, it would be possible to combine 'Environmental studies' with 'Compiling maintenance and operations manuals'. This could be done without BIM, but using BIM techniques environmental information could be structured and its progress and status monitored, managed and quality controlled through project stages so that it automatically formes part of the Building Information Model at the time of handover to the operators and maintenance staff. 'Other Services' and 'Electronic document control system' quoted in the now superseded Schedule of Design Services (SS-DS-07) could still be used in the current appointment as an additional BIM service. The BIM itself could be the electronic system or alternatively, because a BIM approach provides structure, consistency, co-ordination and quality assurance, BIM contents could be ported to some other document system with relative ease. This is valuable.

Another example might be to think of compiling, revising and editing a design brief, writing a 'final brief and room data sheet', in conjunction with compiling maintenance and operational manuals. If the practice is working in a framework agreement with a Clinical Commissioning Group for example, the brief in its final form represents the assumptions and policies behind operating the facility. A BIM methodology would preserve early information and ensure it was in an appropriate form for subsequent use. It is also worth noting that much of this information might be non-graphic, but there is no reason why the same BIM principles should not be applied.

An augmented service for the leading roles – Project Lead, Lead Designer and Contract Administrator – could be promoted using BIM techniques. Any of these positions could act as an information quality control agency provided an extra fee was charged for the additional liability. This could pre-empt the contractor doing the same thing but for different reasons. Claims could be prevented at an early stage instead of being spotted later; this has to command considerable value.

A step further

The potential for BIM to allow larger projects to be undertaken has already been mentioned. When sufficient expertise has been gathered, BIM might be promoted as a management methodology and additional fees might be charged to facilitate and guide the rest of the project team towards a BIM approach. Fees could be charged to the client and to other team players who wanted to adopt a BIM approach. In future new professional expertise will grow around the more advanced ingredients of BIM. An earlier section looked at intelligent objects and parametrics. This is fertile ground for the ambitious practice that wants to be one step ahead and that wants to take an innovative step into the not-so-distant future. There are many openings where objects and parametric objects might be manufactured on behalf of public or private sector clients.

Beware the Code of Conduct

The ARB Code of Conduct is largely untested as far as technology issues in general and BIM in particular are concerned. However, it is interesting to conjecture what might happen. The gravest danger is to oversell what is possible with BIM. This might bring into play certain standards from the Code placing a professional obligation on architects to act with 'integrity' and 'technical competence'. How many interpretations of 'technical' are there, sufficient to begin to include technology in today's world? Further, the Code states that architects should only promote their professional services 'in a truthful and responsible manner'. These standards require architects to promote BIM or the use of BIM techniques to their clients in an honest way. Any misrepresentation of what BIM might do could find the architect in breach of the Code. Alternatively, professing to provide expert BIM advice and services without evidence of specialised knowledge might be a case of attempting to provide expertise beyond which is actually possessed, again a breach of conduct.

As architects, the Code of Conduct directs us not to mislead or purport to offer an expertise we do not have. Architects should ensure there is proper professional competence in BIM if it is being offered as a value-added service. Be wary of sweeping statements such as 'an update in one area of the BIM automatically updates all the drawings'. Apart from enticing the client to request a reduction in fees, does the changed state still conform to Building Regulations, the latest cost report given to the client, fire regulations or energy calculations, for example?

Standard 4.3 of the *Architects Code: Standards of Conduct and Practice* states:

You should ensure that adequate security is in place to safeguard both paper and electronic records for your clients, taking full account of data protection legislation, and that clients' confidential information is safeguarded.

This places a responsibility on architects to protect electronic information in a BIM environment; servers holding client information may be situated at a remote location, in which case the Code places an obligation on the architect to check its security. Further still the advent of cloud computing may mean that the precise location of clients' electronic data is difficult to pinpoint and considerable resource could be absorbed in establishing its whereabouts and safe keeping. Assuming a business savvy architect or architectural practice does define BIM as an additional service then the utmost care should be taken in how the definition of the services is structured and drafted.

▶ SUMMARY

What new business opportunities come with BIM?

- Simple BIM techniques offer business advantage within the office without necessarily involving anyone else.

- Forms of architects' appointment offer a wide range of opportunities for selling value-added services based on BIM. If you see value, charge for it.

- Sell BIM techniques from pre-inception and beyond Final Certificate

- Look for innovation in the way BIM might be applied to the full range of services undertaken.

- Do not fall into the 'spin trap' and oversell BIM in contravention of the ARB Code of Conduct.

SECTION 8
Will our clients want BIM?

Is the client suitable and willing to adopt BIM?

This is another question of scale. The one-off small domestic client will probably not need to be aware of the processes that have to be gone through and the information that has to be produced to achieve the result they want. However, all other clients outside the one-off domestic market might benefit to differing extents from a BIM approach. Many will not understand what it is, what they have to do to achieve advantage or indeed how to participate in a team that uses BIM techniques. Some will have heard a buzz word and what almost amounts to hearsay about advantage. They will want their ounce of flesh from their project team, who they will expect to produce miracles.

An earlier section gave a brief view of some of the initiatives being taken by the US General Services Administration and the State of Wisconsin. In particular the GSA has established a National 3D-4D-BIM Program (General Services Administration 2006) which in part includes educating public and potential service providers in changing how they procure work. Their approach will inevitably spread across the Atlantic and the large commercial and institutional clients in the UK will be making BIM part of their procurement considerations.

Large institutional and private sector clients show a tendency to latch onto these new ideas but not fully understand what is involved. PFI and PPP initiatives are a good example. It has taken many years for these different procurement methods to be recognised as having provided benefit. Indeed there are still those today who would question whether or not success has been achieved. The likelihood is that this type of client may well incorporate some form of BIM requirements in procurement documents. They will require their teams to adopt BIM and cause problems by misunderstanding the framework in which it works. BIM is relatively new and as can be seen from the contents of this book still a movable feast as to what it means.

Yet genuine and reliable experience of and experience in BIM implementation is scarce and the danger is that uninformed individuals on both sides of the procurement counter will have their own possibly flawed interpretations and are likely to waste a great deal of money and cause some pain before getting it right. Ideally the institutional or large private client would allow for a prototype trial. Working with trusted providers on a pilot project would highlight potential trouble spots in procurement documentation, legal and insurance frameworks, technology platforms, clarity of roles and responsibilities and information flows. The cost of this would probably be no more than launching straight into a project using BIM and finding the problems and facing their repercussions as the project progressed. Even worse still, without a pilot project, a commercial relationship that could have prospered breaks down instead.

Some clients may be sceptical about the use of BIM. BIM could be perceived as being in its infancy and many believe this could drive costs upwards. Changing established procurement methods does come at a cost both to purchaser and supplier. If return is not readily demonstrable then doubt will creep in about embarking on a new route. It is the 'I do not want to be the first in the marketplace' syndrome.

What are the benefits for the client?

Considered correctly, BIM can bring benefits to any type of client, whatever the size of their project, whether it is a one-off or repeat project, or whether they are in the private or public sector. The first, and perhaps for many clients the most obvious, benefit is the provision of 3D visualisations which are extracted from the BIM, and which are increasingly being used for numerous practical reasons. For example a virtual prototype might be created to illustrate the installation path of specialist, large or awkward equipment into a hospital suite. Building this visualisation might avoid embarrassing complications part way through construction or may establish that what is envisaged is not feasible. Another practical situation where clients could benefit is maintenance access. Difficult ceiling voids or restricted areas for plant can be modelled in 1:1 accurate detail so that maintenance checks can be carried out comfortably and health and safety regulations adhered to.

Simulating construction sequencing can deliver a client's facility earlier and ensure expensive capital is working as soon as possible. Modelling construction phases and sequences can also form the basis of a financial borrowing draw-down programme, ensuring interest charges are kept to a minimum. Fit first time, off-site manufacture, lean construction, just-in-time inventory based on a well co-ordinated, quality controlled information model can all play their part more effectively in a BIM context.

For some clients the manufacture of a long term information asset is of enormous value. The utilities, hospital sites, university sites, Ministry of Defence projects and airports are just a few examples where a high quality information base has a different but equivalent value to the facility itself. For example, accurate floor area data passed on to facility managers has a high value in obtaining quotes and contracts for cleaning and redecoration. Locations and performance specifications of plant, machinery and equipment are extremely useful for planned and reactive maintenance. Crowd simulations and evacuation procedures are quickly becoming available, albeit perhaps as yet another specialist additional software package in an already crowded BIM software environment.

Are there costs to the client? – yes and no

Whether there are any costs to the client is a business decision with several facets.

BIM can be an internal efficiency strategy and the fact that BIM methodologies are being adopted need not be disclosed to the client. The business simply works in better ways to improve its own bottom line. In this sense there is no direct or noticeable cost to the client.

This approach might be adopted with clients who have no interest in BIM or the 'lay' client who has no knowledge of how the architect works in their own office or with the wider team. However the office implements BIM in this context, any capital or revenue costs to the business due to a strategic investment in BIM will be reflected in internal cost structures and the fee level offered to the client. For clients who want to generate benefits from BIM, modifications to workflows and alterations to procurement methods and documentation will incur additional cost. For the conscientious client who wants to be well informed and who wants to play a positive role in a BIM environment, they too should invest in BIM and/or information management training. Clients for whom information might be a company investment and asset should be prepared to incur extra cost in the form of purchasing an additional value-added service spelt out in the form of an additional service defined in the form of appointment.

A new stimulus from Government

The report for the Government Construction Client Group published in March 2011 should be a major stimulus in encouraging the public sector client down the BIM route. The report illustrates a long term commitment that could benefit all stakeholders. The fact that the report provokes interest in better information and a more co-operative environment is a very good thing. Most if not all it proposes are necessary steps for architecture and construction irrespective of whether the BIM acronym had appeared or not.

Education on both sides of the counter

Given the interest in BIM the key thing to get right is education. Both purchaser and provider must be well informed about which BIM ingredients are being purchased and they must have a clear understanding of what they are asking for and why. The danger is that the Government procurement client can be populated with those who have no qualification in architecture and construction. As a consequence they can be quite easily misled by those with vested interests. The procurement paradigm is then in danger of becoming a distorted process with unreasonable expectations by all parties of the outcome.

The Government client should also be aware of paying for added value, provided it gets an information asset as a tangible result of the procurement process. BIM is not and should not be seen simply as a vehicle for forcing prices down. The concepts surrounding BIM need to be acknowledged in the educational system at all levels; higher education, Continuing Professional Development (CPD) programmes and professional institution recognition. The concepts being discussed under the BIM banner are worthy of a higher education course in their own right.

If BIM is to be successful then the education question has to be the top priority to avoid the misunderstandings and misrepresentations that were present in the early days of CAD. More than that, the most important people to focus on are the strategy makers, again on both sides of the counter.

An information asset in the context of the public client has an important part to play as a national resource with a long life provided the information base is properly maintained over time. To achieve an information base that can be trusted by everyone who uses and contributes to it, it has to be produced in an environment where the overriding interest is the information asset and not the individual business interests of those who produced it. This is unlikely to be achieved under the traditional forms of adversarial contract and procurement that encourage protectionism.

BIM should be viewed as a 'national business plan' in the sense of the business plan idea described previously. There should be a first phase of investment/possible loss in education and training research into what a model procurement document should contain. A second break-even phase follows where new BIM concepts can be implemented and evaluated and finally a third phase when hopefully the benefits to the public purse and private enterprise can be felt. Other topics such as digital capabilities, technology, whole life costing and carbon performance will naturally follow, if the educational and legal context is well formed.

> ▶ **SUMMARY**

Will our clients want BIM?

- The domestic client may well be unaware of BIM techniques and therefore will not be interested.

- The UK and USA are introducing BIM clauses into procurement documents.

- 'Folklore' on both sides of the BIM counter will hinder the realisation of BIM benefits.

- 3D BIM can provide many practical design insights as well as better management of client finance.

- Any large scale client who manages an information asset could benefit from a project team operating BIM methodologies.

- The Government client will play an important part in rolling out BIM.

SECTION 9
BIM in the supply chain

The supply chain contributes a significant amount of information

Perhaps the current BIM movement will create a different outlook towards the supply chain.

With some enlightened exceptions the perception is that the relationship between the supply chain and the rest of the design/construct professionals suffers from poor communication, is full of mistrust and contributes to the blame culture. Furthermore, because of the high degree of fragmentation in the industry or, put another way, because of the many components and materials there are, the supply chain creates waste, inefficiencies and uncertainty.

This may be a little unfair on the supply chain given the presence of the contractor in the gap between design and the finished article. The quest for lowest construction cost often denies design intention and has implications for operating expenditure.

Whether this perception is right or wrong it needs to be re-engineered into a more positive form because the supply chain plays a crucial part in creating the built environment.

With some exceptions the supply chain consists predominantly of SMEs. They come together in supply chain form to produce a whole which is greater than the sum of its parts. As with all SMEs in this BIM movement the supply chain SMEs can adjust quickly to take advantage of BIM benefits.

Given a co-operative outlook within the project team the advantages to the supply chain and the ultimate outcome are:

- Enhanced value propositions in the marketplace.
- Reduced cycle times for design and production.
- Potential elimination of co-ordination errors.
- Lower costs due to a more informed involvement.
- In some cases the delivery of data to drive automated manufacture and off-site production.
- Lean inventory and just-in-time delivery.

The key to exploiting these advantages lies in the supply chain being involved as soon as is appropriate. Obviously, to involve all supply chain members would be difficult to manage, but any project will have its bias or emphasis towards a smaller subset. A key factor is that projects are managed in a truly collaborative environment with a fully integrated project team.

For example, the aspiration to conserve energy might involve organisations who supply the external skin of a facility and those who install energy sources, whatever their basis, ranging from sophisticated systems to renewable sources of energy. Their involvement might include, for instance, advice on thermal performance at early design stages and maintainability post completion.

Involving the supply chain is more a question of BIM the culture rather than BIM the technology. In other words the technology which would support the early involvement of the supply chain, its information and its persistence through to post Final Certificate use has been there for some time.

It is the cultural change that BIM symbolises that would empower the supply chain to play a more significant role. After all its members are the ones who know most about their products, how they are produced and how they might best be used.

Engaging the supply chain

At one level the supply chain has expressed an enthusiasm for getting involved by their presence at the national launch of the BIM Regional Hubs. This is most welcome and their enquiries as to how to make a contribution is encouraging.

When talking about BIM it is necessary to establish which ingredients are being spoken of and the scale of the organisation engaged in the dialogue. There are different conversations and paces of BIM adoption and use when talking to different sizes of organisation with differing obligations. The supply chain is rich in variety, from those who design, create, manufacture and install sophisticated components to those who are adept at manual skills acquired over many years of experience.

That range of knowledge and expertise requires an appropriate BIM interaction. Some need a high degree of technical information from the design team to be able to provide their product. Others require minimal information to carry out their particular craft, trade or ingenuity.

All are valid and require information carefully honed to their needs, which may be complex or simple. In return they should contribute information which supports their product's characteristic performance throughout project life cycle.

The product supplier's dilemma (specification versus contractor buying cheapest)

'Or similar' on drawings, models or specification documents are dreaded words as far as some product suppliers are concerned. The product manufacturer would like to see their product embedded into the project team's and contractor's psyche. Traditionally the architect could retain control of product specification. However, increasingly, especially with the rise of more and more design and build type procurement routes, the power of doing this has passed to the contractor, who will enhance their own profit margins by purchasing the nearest but cheapest thing thanks to those dreaded words.

Most products and materials on the market have a vast range of characteristics that have to be taken into account for various design, construction and operational purposes. The product provider could organise these characteristics, or property sets in the jargon of COBie and Ifc, into groups that are useful to the various actors in project life cycle. This makes the stakeholder's life easier and perhaps makes them more inclined to use that particular product.

For example, headings for property sets might be: design criteria, assembly instructions, maintenance guidance, fire protection performance, installation instructions, redecoration requirements, energy performance, CO_2 characteristics. The list is endless and there is no overall standard list, each generic type of product has its own set of property sets.

The product supplier has the option of giving this information away free of charge in the hope that does the trick. Alternatively they may regard it as a new value proposition and promote the idea that there is a ready-made database for their product that is useful throughout project life cycle, in which case it should be purchased. The choice is theirs.

This is not a guaranteed proposition of course, but if product manufacturers and supply chain members want the best chance of surety, then this is it. Those who take advantage of this approach may steal a march on their competitors and contractors in the short to medium term.

BIM education in the supply chain

From the beginning the Government BIM initiative has placed great emphasis on engaging the supply chain. Not only are there commercial considerations to be taken into account to get them involved, but the supply chain needs to be made aware of the significance of the information it supplies and requires, so that all parties benefit throughout project life cycle.

The vast range of suppliers presents a challenge to those wanting to educate. To achieve this aim, information must be fine tuned and the form and content shaped for individuals.

Indeed, who can the educators of the supply chain be? There is a big question mark over whether the supply chain is ready to accept and use BIM. A glance into several corners of the construction industry reveals a spectrum of outlooks.

The definition of the supply chain is as elusive as the interpretation of the BIM acronym itself. There needs to be clarification of what is being spoken of when referring to the supply chain. The usual perception is the immediate members of the project team and the product suppliers and manufacturers who provide the fabric and contents of what is being built. This is a broad enough church to contemplate education, but it does not stop there. A wider view of the supply chain might include building control officers, planners, solicitors and health and safety officers. Their information has a significant influence on the built facility and should be fully incorporated into the BIM environment.

The pedagogic model for this broad expanse of education needs to be as rich and diverse as the construction industry itself. Higher education, further education, vocational courses in-service training, sandwich courses, office-based programmes in conjunction with education establishments and many more educational paradigms will have to play a part in the colossal task of bringing along everyone in the supply chain.

A pan industry pedagogic structure which delivers an integrated education package with BIM at the heart of the subject domain would be a profound new world. It would provide a BIM-focused education with overlaps into other areas of technology, business, law and regulation, for example, as opposed to BIM being an 'add on' to already established courses. The ambition to change culture by 2016 provokes a gigantic educational challenge if the 'community of five million' in construction is to be educated in a different way.

▶ **SUMMARY**

BIM in the supply chain

• The supply chain's engagement in terms of expertise and authoritative information is essential to the future of BIM and cultural change in the construction industry.

• Greater involvement of the supply chain early on is critical to decision making which has repercussions throughout project life cycle.

• The supply chain has opportunities to provide new value propositions within BIM.

• Involving the supply chain is more a question of BIM culture than technology.

• Incorporating the vast number of people involved in the supply chain into the BIM environment creates new challenges for education, training and support.

SECTION 10
How do we implement BIM?

Previous discussion in this book has shown that BIM is an adaptable concept depending on an individual or collective viewpoint in any size of practice. The intention of this section is to give those who want to progress their BIM endeavour to some extent a practical and pragmatic way of going about it. There is no right or wrong way. There is no complete BIM or BIM methodology. Every practice and project team must adopt and adapt what it believes to be right for itself. As a consequence embedded culture will inevitably change.

The following suggestions represent a set of principles that can be implemented by an individual, an individual practice, a group within a practice or a complete project team encompassing many companies. The sections are written so that no matter what scale you operate at you can choose which series of metrics you wish to adopt in your implementation of a BIM strategy. At this stage the assumption is that the business case for embarking on a BIM approach has been made; the emphasis here is on implementing BIM not the reasons for doing so. The metrics tables are intended as a guide. Generally, moving from left to right in the tables indicates the possibility of reaching a more collaborative state either for the individual, the practice or the project team. The more rows that can be absorbed successfully into working practices the more there is a likelihood of BIM success.

BIM metrics – choosing the individual

People are the greatest asset in any practice and success depends on getting the right people for the job. BIM is no exception. For architects the ARB Code of Conduct is a good starting point for the value system required by BIM working. Standard 1 of the Code insists that architects act with 'honesty and integrity' and goes on to say that no statement should be made that is 'misleading' or 'unfair to others' and that conflicts of interest should be disclosed. These sentiments are absolutely in line with functioning in a co-operative atmosphere. The co-operative member of staff must be prepared to lead when necessary as well as support the leadership of others. Behaviour should aim towards the accomplishment of work tasks and support the relationships between team members. There must also be an acceptance of what working with other team members is meant to achieve.

Values	Non co-operation			Co-operation
Collaborative experience	No collaborative experience	Minimal collaborative experience under duress	Minimal collaborative experience but seeks more opportunities	Only ever had collaborative experiences
Attitude to standards and protocols	Believes standards and protocols inhibit working methods	Has own standards and protocols and unwilling to change	Will reluctantly adopt standards and protocols of others	Believes standards and protocols enable better communications hence better project results
Flexibility	Cynical	Give it a try under duress	Open minded to gain new experience	Will adapt to any project situation
Teamwork	Isolationist	Work in teams under coercion	Work in teams when possible to learn something new	Will only work in collaborative teams

FIGURE 10.1 Indicative metric for choosing the individual.

Creative thinking in the application of BIM principles to new situations is a tremendous asset in a human resource when attempting to solve unfamiliar problems with people who are hesitant in facing change. Obviously an ability to use the various types of software commonly found in a BIM context is an advantage but care should be taken that the individual has genuine knowledge about the software she/he says they can manipulate. Enquiry into the technical concepts embodied in systems rather than twenty questions on tips and tricks will reveal whether an individual really understands what any software platform can contribute.

For example, an individual might be asked what part the concept of a layer or level might play in avoiding litigation. A question like this probes the business and project understanding of how powerful information structuring and management devices found in software platforms can be used to serious advantage. A non-partisan attitude towards software platforms, portals and information standards is essential. Any technological technique can assist collaborative working if the parties involved want it to. The traditional outlook of 'my system is better than yours' gets the team nowhere.

Probing the individual's approach to storing information on their own computer is one example of exposing strengths or weaknesses in how they might manage information in a more collaborative context. A reluctance to accommodate document management conventions on the grounds that it is an extra burden to learn in a busy office probably indicates someone who might struggle in a BIM context. The person who realises that such conventions are a means of helping the whole office during times of high-pressure working, staff absence or continuity of working on jobs is, on the other hand, likely to be a useful asset.

BIM metrics – choosing the company

	Non co-operation			Co-operation
Champions	No champions	Enthusiastic individuals in project team/s	Some champions at the top table	All top table are champions
Policy	No policy on collaboration	Collaboration happens by being drawn into legal arrangements	Collaboration is being trialled on selected projects	Collaboration is a company policy supported at the highest level
Experience	No collaborative experience	Minimal collaborative experience under duress	Minimal collaborative experience but seeking other opportunities	Only ever had collaborative experiences
Technology	Technology is not part of business strategy	Technology used giving isolated business advantage	Some aspects of technology used in an integrated way for business advantage	All aspects of technology integrated into business strategy
Information standards	No information standard, each individual left to their own devices	Company information standard exists but is used inconsistently	Company information standard implemented as policy	Industry information standard implemented as company policy
Flexibility	Cynical	Give it a try under duress	Open minded to gain new experience	Will adapt to any project situation
Teamwork	Isolationist	Work in teams because of legal obligations	Work in teams when possible to learn something new	Only work in collaborative teams
Innovation	Not willing to change	Have had to change	Want to change	Always looking for ways to change for the better
Openness	Protectionist attitude towards finance and IPR	Provide openness because of legal obligation	Want to increase openness when opportunity arises	Openness creates advantage for all
Project vision	Own business interest comes first	Compromise under duress	Compromise is first port of call	Project interests come first

continued

continued	Non co-operation		Co-operation	
Blame	It is always someone else's fault	Mediation, adjudication	Willing to share pain/gain	No-blame culture
Contracts	Only use adversarial forms of contract	Been part of framework or partnering arrangements through commercial necessity	Looking for more opportunities to use collaborative forms of contract	Only use collaborative forms of contract

FIGURE 10.2 Indicative metric for choosing the company.

Not every practice is willing to or capable of making the shift towards BIM. Selection has to be carried out carefully to identify those who are genuinely interested in change and the advantages BIM has to offer. Often the first reaction is that BIM is a means of applying pressure to cut costs. BIM can result in a reduction in costs if that is a criterion the team aspires to meet, but lesser cost has to be a shared objective and carried out for the right reasons.

In 1860 John Ruskin said 'It is unwise to pay too much, but it is worse to pay too little. When you pay too much you lose a little money that is all. When you pay too little, you sometimes lose everything, because the thing you bought was incapable of doing the thing it was bought to do. The common law of business balance prohibits paying a little and getting a lot, it cannot be done. If you deal with the lowest bidder, it is well to add something for the risk you run. And, if you do that, you will have enough to pay for something better.' Mr Ruskin anticipated the attitude of many of those involved in modern day construction whose only but often misplaced motive is to save on cost.

Champions

Perhaps the most important factor in assessing whether a practice will be an acceptable BIM participant is to know that it has champions at the top table. If it has, there may be a double bonus in that these individuals not only champion the BIM cause but also know what is involved in terms of technology, information management and process change and what the implications are. Alternatively, they may not have all this knowledge at their disposal but nevertheless an enlightened instinct, coupled with an enquiring mind and a listening ear with trusted staff that do, is just as valuable.

Champions can have a varying degree of influence. It may be that they are in a minority but with firmly held beliefs. Often their colleagues at high level will tolerate their views and show interest on occasions but really they believe there are more important things the business should be concentrating on. Nevertheless the committed champion never goes away and will over a period of time make a difference.

Policy

A better position is if BIM can be embedded in policy. Edicts can be a good thing if properly formulated, resourced and implemented.

Experience

Testing the practice for its BIM credentials can extend to asking questions about how it treats those it works with and how it engenders a co-operative atmosphere. Evidence of working in framework agreements, partnering relationships, open book accounting, KPIs and programmes for continuous improvement will be important indicators for BIM readiness.

Technology and information standards

The company's attitude towards information technology will be revealing. It should have what it might call a 'CAD standard'. This may be based on a recognised standard such as BS 1192; it may well be a variation of this or a completely home grown orthodoxy but its presence and contents can be used as an indicator on the readiness or otherwise to conform to a paradigm for organising information. The approach to technology and information will display two important things; first, a company-wide attitude to BIM and second, the practical ability to enter into a wider project team context using BIM. In the first instance a good regime for technology and information standards indicates a culture where a proper move towards BIM has and continues to take place. It shows that BIM is part of a business case within the company and to some extent at least has backing at senior level. When that company enters a project team it can either become a BIM leader to convert others or use its knowledge to interface its information successfully with team players who may have a different BIM outlook or none at all.

Flexibility

In a BIM environment any practice or project team, no matter what the size, has to contemplate changes in business process. Analysing operational activity and observing where strengths and weaknesses lie is essential if a new business/project model is to emerge. There is a trade-off between the overhead incurred in examining working practices and the implementation of new procedures. A previous section discusses the business case for BIM and restructuring processes is a critical element in what should be incorporated into a budget for a BIM strategy.

Teamwork

It takes a special kind of person to genuinely work in a team. There is a need to be assertive and restrained, sometimes lead, sometimes follow. An authentic willingness to want to understand how others work in order to work well with them is paramount. Teamwork can be summarised by the saying 'the whole is greater than the sum of its parts'. If the combined expertise of a team can work in harmony without being concerned about who takes credit or blame, then a different order of magnitude of benefit all round can be achieved.

Innovation

Change to the new or different almost always engenders scepticism and resistance to some extent. Even worse, fear of innovation can breed a form of innovation paralysis. Simple change management techniques should be employed to get individuals from where they are to a new position. The key is always to involve people and be clear about what and why change could or should take place.

Openness

Openness should involve a breadth of thought, a non-partisan outlook and frankness about moving to a different way of working. Either the individual business or the project team, involving several sets of business interests, can agree to operate a version of open book accounting as it were, in order to establish a BIM protocol. The term would not simply apply to the arithmetic of finance but also to people issues such as roles and responsibilities.

If things go wrong – don't blame

It is easy to cast blame when things do not go according to plan; the contractor, the supply chain, the changes in client requirements and the fallibility of the architect can all be held responsible. Blame forces individuals to go on the defensive; it generates unnecessary paperwork, anxiety and resentments. Things will go wrong and, provided there is no malicious intent, then a BIM environment taken with a more co-operative legal framework should enable shared responsibility and risk. Blame is eliminated by adopting and supporting clear responsibilities and using the BIM environment to enable integrated communication.

Contracts

Modern forms of contract are trying to provide a legal backdrop for a more collaborative approach which is essential in a BIM context. Section 11 looks at this in greater detail.

BIM metrics – auditing the project team

	Non co-operation			Co-operation
Positioning information	No common orientation No common origin A mixture of positive and negative co-ordinates No common grid			Common orientation Common origin Positive co-ordinates Common grid
Measurement	No common units Eyeball dimensioning No common scale			Common units Automatic dimensioning Common scale – 1:1
Information conventions	No conventions	Disparate conventions	Disparate conventions but managed	Common convention throughout the project team
Software platform	Disparate platforms			Disparate platforms but managed
Portal	Disparate portals			Disparate portals but managed
Operational extent	Core project team	Extended core project team	+ supply chain	+ project life cycle players
Roles and responsibilities	Not defined	Defined but not common	Some commonality	Commonality
Processes	Not defined	Defined but not common	Some commonality	Commonality
Legal arrangements	Adversarial		Positive	Collaborative
Insurance arrangements	Individual professional indemnity insurance			Single project insurance

FIGURE 10.3 Indicative metric for auditing the project team.

The team comes together

The BIM team should be brought together at the earliest opportunity. If the tables above have been used as a guide then the team has already given a preliminary indication of their ability and willingness to participate in a BIM initiative. The starting point for BIM strategy on a project is not always clear; particular projects may demand that the core team be in place, others may require the lead consultant to develop the BIM protocol, or the client may provide/require one. In any instance it is best to start as early as possible but to be cognisant of others who will join the project team and the BIM as the project develops.

The emergence of the core team will most likely be a signal that the broad outline of the project is visible, in which case extensions to the core team and likely involvement of supply chains can be estimated. If there are significant players identified in this wider community they should be included in the next stages of assembling the BIM strategy.

Audit the team

Once the core and as many of the extended core team members as is thought necessary have been identified then a comprehensive audit should be carried out. The real work of working in BIM mode begins. Auditing the team is a crucial activity with several interrelated facets to its implementation. Interview and references of previous BIM working, if any, will provide a preliminary indication of who is keen to perform differently and co-operatively. This fact-finding mission should include senior management, all levels of staff likely to have an involvement and the CAD manager.

Lip service answers given at this stage will be exposed when it comes to signing up for a different set of legal arrangements surrounding BIM; arrangements that should clearly define what every party's obligations to the BIM are. Having carried out a preliminary assessment of their BIM potential the assembled team will need to be reminded to be rigorous about their BIM methodology and to be aware of risks and responsibilities.
The motives for this are usually mixed. Some may be genuinely overenthusiastic about what they can do, others bluff their way hoping that technology-speak will see them through. Fear and embarrassment factors too play their part in an inaccurate calibration of expertise. Fear among individuals, especially senior managers of practices, means that they are frightened to declare they do not know as much as they believe others do. Embarrassment can inhibit proper potential to be displayed because of a reluctance to ask questions about what is not understood.

Facilitating the team

Facilitating the audit via an experienced third party is the best way of avoiding partisan view points, conflicts of personality and clashes of practice positions. The facilitator can ask incisive questions, perhaps the questions that people are frightened to ask. The aim is to tease out what can really be achieved in terms of a BIM. It is important to get a programme of workshops agreed, with senior managers' input to these occasions being absolutely essential.

Audit the process

The team is asked to step through the processes they anticipate will take them from the starting point of being brought together to the end point of the collaborative BIM project indicated by the RIBA work stages 0 to 6 Inception to Final Certificate. This process will take several sessions operating at different levels. For example, a large property development organisation might be looking to embrace BIM within its organisation. A workshop of twenty or thirty people including company directors, accountants, surveyors, architects, M&E engineers, structural engineers, letting agents and PR consultants might be asked to step through a typical project in twelve easy moves. The first unassuming question might be, 'Who starts the project'? Perhaps three people believe they do.

The capital projects manager believes it is him because no project starts without being approved on the capital programme and that is his responsibility. The surveyor believes it is her because she is the first person on the new site, gathering measured and other information. The architect believes it is him because he puts together the first design ideas. In this scenario there will inevitably be a duplication of information and effort, which will also be collected in disparate places and structure. This has a cost to the organisation. It is then possible for the company to implement a co-ordinated approach to the start of a project. This form of analysis can be adopted from inception to completion and the company can assess for itself what bottom-line saving there might be.

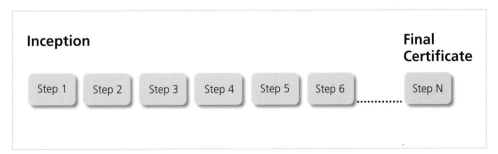

FIGURE 10.4 A high level process.

It may be necessary to variously work with individuals in the team, one company at a time or collectively. The next audit step depends on the outcome from the previous; it has to be a fluid situation. Members at all levels should be available for facilitated workshop sessions, it is a good idea to mix hierarchical levels because it may be one of the few chances people have of saying what they think they should be doing and other people hearing what they are doing. This is often revealing when managers are heard to say 'I didn't realise they were doing that' or 'they shouldn't be doing that now'. These and many similar comments have been heard in workshop sessions.

It is part of the self-educational process in embarking on a BIM trajectory. BIM or no BIM, it is enlightening to compare notes from time to time. More important is the mix of policy, technology and process perceptions that emerge. They are useful for checking practice or project direction in any case, but form the foundations of being able to achieve a successful BIM environment. Processes, roles and responsibilities grow into folklore over time and tend to deviate from the policies which senior managers have spelt out. Checking and adjusting is cathartic and essential. The basic procedure is simple and that is to ask each member of the team:

- What information do they expect to receive at the start of the process?
- What information do they expect to be the output from the process?
- Who are the players in the process?
- What are the constraints on that particular process?

Constraints in particular could be a high level sign-off event, a planning approval, an agreement on brief content with a client, or a Practical Completion Certificate. The levels of agreement and disagreement are a very important part of revealing what the true nature of the problem is for getting people to work together collaboratively within a BIM context. The conversation will inevitably require a drill down into more detail for each stage, and it may be necessary to gain executive permission to push people to say in confidence exactly what is on their mind in terms of being able to achieve the BIM objective. It requires a rather brave senior manager to assent to this because inadequacies of management can be exposed or weaknesses in policy implementation identified.

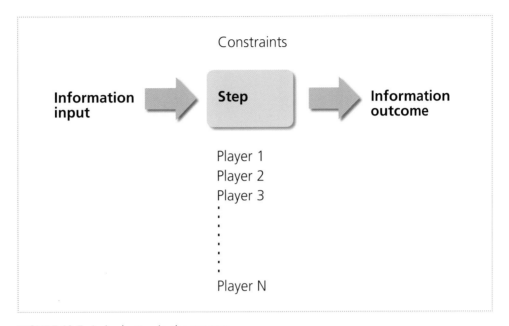

FIGURE 10.5 A single step in the process.

When facilitation is complete the team should have a common view of the who, when and what they are doing from beginning to end of their particular project work. The process framework is then used to probe deeper in to other significant and related topics. The outcome of the analysis is to gain a series of work flows that can be agreed upon by the team. It might be expedient to propose adjustments to this process framework at this stage.

Audit roles and responsibilities

What people do under the title they possess varies enormously. Even when the same words are used in a job title, the job description can extend in many different directions. Even then, what people actually do on the ground can deviate significantly from the text of the description. Converging on a common understanding of what people do shapes the BIM environment.

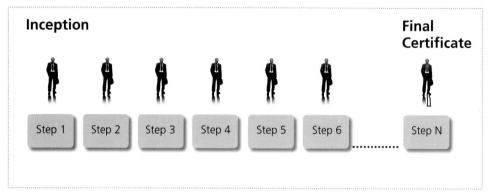

FIGURE 10.6 A common understanding of what people do.

Audit software

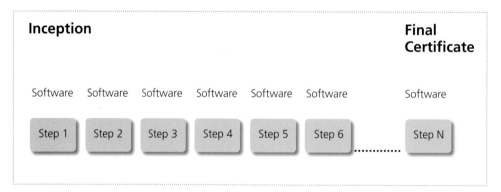

FIGURE 10.7 Which software platform?

In a BIM world, software platforms are the next device to come under the microscope. At each of the identified process stages every team member declares which software platform they will use. Other cans of worms are opened in that there will be, as might be expected, several software systems used by the team. Again this usually proves to be fertile ground for exchanging domains of expertise and knowledge. The software audit is an occasion when technology can meet business and the partner/director/workstation user divide can be addressed directly. These workshops are most effective if kept at a conceptual level rather than delving deep into technology pea soup.

Every team member should declare the software package they intend to use in the BIM. There is no single package that covers every aspect of small or large scale projects. Indeed different consultant and supply chain functions inevitably call for different software platforms. Structures, HVAC, asset management, visualisations and concept design have all spawned their own specific packages or a component in an extensive software suite.

Collaborative portals can add to the confusion. There are several on the market and larger firms have made their investment in the one they believe suits them best. The downside is that companies obviously tend to take a partisan stance to the one they have bought. As with any software platform, changing or collecting different ones consumes time and money. In a philosophical sense using more than one of these systems ironically runs counter to what they are trying to achieve.

What's your version?

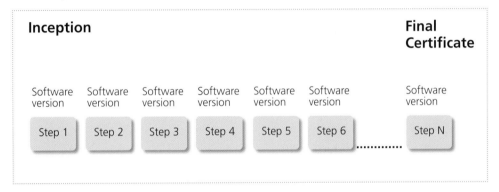

FIGURE 10.8 Which software version?

It would be impossible to expect every member of the team to unite around one common version of one software platform. The version of each software component has to be taken into account. Many a frustrating hour is spent by CAD managers and professionals using a workstation on trying to 'beat the system' by passing their information between different versions of the same software only to find that it did not work. Backwards compatibility between versions is a perennial and serious problem.

On short term projects people may not be prepared at that particular moment to upgrade or change version. Upgrading involves some expenditure probably in terms of increased licence fees and possibly minor changes to working methods. Alternatively an update to a newer version can present newer possibilities for BIM and for offering value-added services.

On long term projects new versions could pose problems with legacy data. There will be a time when software vendors produce points of no turning back. For the average practice this will probably not be problematical, but any organisation with a long term large scale database representing their property portfolio will have to consider what 'no turning back' means. Rarely is data lost because of this, but new techniques may mean that some data may not be able to be manipulated as it had been previously.

Version upgrades should be consciously planned and their implications thoroughly understood. They should not be adopted because of sales pressure or special offers from vendors, or because of a sense of wanting to keep up with someone else. New software versions should be phased in gently to tease out any problems with workflows and implications for the management of existing and future project information.

Audit information conventions

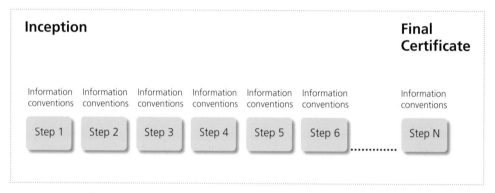

FIGURE 10.9 Information conventions.

Information standards are a key factor in the successful operation of a BIM environment. It is not an attractive subject as far as the vast majority of practitioners are concerned. If only the benefits could be appreciated then architecture and construction might enjoy a contribution to profitability that many other industries have readily absorbed into their armoury of competitiveness and efficiency.

Generally individuals and individual practices have their own way of keeping information on their computers. Asked if they have a standard, representatives from any practice may well say, yes we have one. Closer inspection will show that not only will there be variations within the practice but the chances of two or more practices agreeing a standard are as remote as the farthest galaxy.

What do we mean when we say 'information standard' in a BIM context? Graphic and non-graphic information will be generated from many software sources. Basically there are three devices at our disposal to identify where information is kept, who owns it and what it represents. They are folder name, file name and file content structure. Secondary considerations like validity or status are qualifiers which can be added.

Folders or directories are used every day by almost anyone who uses a computer. Folders are an extremely powerful invention greatly underused and misunderstood. Most of us give our folders names that have significance to ourselves. Provided we understand the shorthand names we have used then adding more information and retrieving what we want is straightforward. The folder structure itself need not be understood by anyone else. If we give a file to someone they will absorb it into their folder structure wherever it makes sense to them; if we receive a file, we will do likewise.

Files names follow similar ideas. In the personal world of our laptop or desktop we can give a file any name we please. It can be terse or flamboyant provided it has a meaning to the individual who authored it.

The contents of files, especially those generated by graphic systems, are just as likely to be individually organised. In a BIM environment a highly personalised and idiosyncratic view is unhelpful and would lead to a great deal of confusion as to where information was kept, who authored it and what state it was in. At best this means confusion and miscommunication, at worst it leads to litigation. Graphic and non-graphic file contents are at the heart of BIM. Any form of inaccuracy or lack of co-ordination could lead to a whole plethora of consequences: lost revenues, premature interest payments, loss of profit, contravention of regulations, components that do not fit together properly, contractual claims and contravention of PI insurance cover; the list is endless and with serious consequences.

As a profession we need to get out of the mindset that creating consistent information within teams is an inconvenience and expensive. Surely it makes sense for the benefit of the project if everyone has a common understanding, and maximum use of the same information. Too often information is compiled on a 'use once only' basis for the occasions when the team gets together, only to be regenerated and discarded when the group goes back to their respective bases. Information should be constantly available for use by all on a day-to-day basis and in a form that everyone has signed up to. In our information-inefficient world there is a tendency to heap everything into one 'drawing', in the hope that what everyone wants is there somewhere and if it is then I must have fulfilled my obligations to my fellow team members. Instead the collective BIM mind could focus on information domains over time, in other words produce the minimum amount for the maximum benefit to key individuals at the time they need it; a kind of just-in-time inventory for information.

Folder and file naming conventions and file content structure are the means at the moment by which we can achieve the best and most influential use of project team information on any project, large or small. This is one of the low cost, low disruption, low investment options mainstream practice has at its disposal to gain benefit from adopting BIM principles.

Exchanging Information

No single computer application will support all the activities associated with BIM, but information does have to be circulated to any player who needs it. Terminology surrounding information exchange can be as confused and misleading, as was earlier suggested when interpreting acronyms such as CAD or BIM.

What sort of information?

Most architects take for granted the different types of information that we generate whilst carrying out our design and construction activities. Images, text and calculations are copied and pasted and somehow the 3D dimensional 'models' that we show our clients get moved from one place to another. Behind the scenes some quite complicated work has to be done to achieve what we currently have at our disposal to share information. In some respects text is relatively straightforward. Text exchanges rarely lose the text itself but the document or page may well look different when it comes out the other end because the features which determine its appearance may be supported differently on either side of the exchange.

Images too are relatively uncomplicated. When exchanging pixels less can be turned into more but quality and sharpness will not be created. 3D volumes which are generated can be joined together to make more complicated volumes. Whether they retain or discard their original constituents adds further information exchange issues. If we want a 'there and back' exchange does the second system retain the constituent parts so that the original system gets them back and can manipulate them on its own terms again? Do we need two methods of exchange? One where the constituent ingredients are kept and another where they are lost. All methods have their applications, advantages and disadvantages.

The next level of complexity in exchanging information might be objects. An earlier section gave a working concept of what an object is, namely a container for information and the capability to do things. The information it contains could be thought of as a combination of text and geometry and, as described above, there can be considerable problems if this is not exchanged properly. Exchanging 'doing something' or behaviour is much more difficult to achieve between software platforms.

An object might do something with its own information, for example perform a calculation or check one piece of information against another, in which case it has a self-contained action. Alternatively it might have a relationship with one other or many other objects. Therefore ensuring any pair of systems has a mutual understanding of the object, its contents, behaviour and relationships with other objects becomes an area of considerable complexity. Just thinking of the word door will conjure up as many interpretations as people who are asked. Does the idea include, for example, leaf, ironmongery, lining, stops, architrave, special treatments, final finish, electronic equipment and signage? 'Door' might have a relationship with a wall, a light switch, a structural opening, a floor, a ceiling, a fire compartment, structure or furniture. Whether all these forms of information can be successfully exchanged depends on how well and to what extent the software developers want to collaborate and have collaborated.

How do we exchange information?

Passing information around the project team will typically be carried out in one of the two following ways:

Direct proprietary links

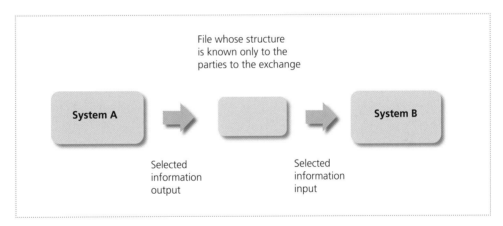

FIGURE 10.10 Proprietary links.

Direct proprietary links are manufactured by two organisations who might exchange data on a regular basis. They may not want anyone else to know what information they are exchanging or how they are doing it. The functions they carry out may involve specialist expertise and therefore what they do is not covered by standard public exchange methods. This method requires each end of the exchange to divulge some level of trade secret as to how their respective information is structured so that the transfer software can do its job reliably. The two organisations involved can develop this at the pace they require; they determine the functionality and supporting it well is in their interests.

Public exchange formats

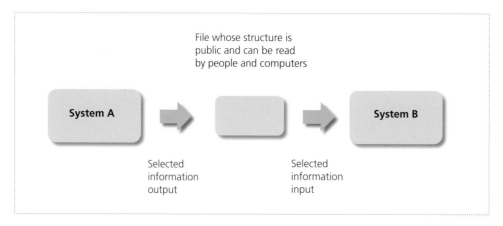

File whose structure is public and can be read by people and computers

System A

System B

Selected information output

Selected information input

FIGURE 10.11 Public exchange formats.

The first organisation keeps its own information structure secret, but writes software that can output an information selection to a file which is structured in an independent public format available to anyone. The second organisation writes software that can absorb the same selection based on the rules of the public structure. All being well information crosses the great divide. Public formats are useful in that, in theory, they can be used to manufacture information exchange software by any pair of industry players in the BIM environment. What functionality is supported by the public format has a direct effect on what information can be exchanged.

The most popularly known exchange formats in this category are DXF and DWG. DXF has been around for thirty years or so and it was developed by Autodesk. It was intended to provide a public representation of the internal data stored in an Autodesk drawing file. It was developed before Autodesk and Bentley agreed to write a form of DWG standard that would serve as a common exchange format in situations where their systems met. This has proved to be useful and pragmatic for many information exchanges but does not yet extend to the sophistication that could be present in a BIM environment and unfortunately does not yet cover all the possible software combinations that might be present in a BIM.

And that horrible, foreboding but much used word, interoperability

The term interoperability is used to cover a multitude of sins. It often used to mean the entire range of possibilities in transferring information between systems of any type. Here, interoperability will be construed as having a quite specific set of characteristics. Proper interoperability is more akin to a copy and paste process. In Microsoft Office an image can be copied and pasted from Access to PowerPoint to Word to Excel. There is no loss, corruption or absence of information. Each part of the Office suite copies information to the clipboard and the receiving part of the suite immediately recognises what it has been sent. There is no damaging effect on the information.

Under the Microsoft 'umbrella' a whole host of objects containing information and behaviour are taken care of within this process. But, instead of an image in the Microsoft suite imagine a package of information in an equivalent architectural context. Suppose a structural steel layout or cladding solution or an HVAC network could be copied and pasted in the same way. Objects in the sending system prepare the 'copy' and objects in the receiving system accept the 'paste'. Objects that manage relationships would check that whatever had been pasted fits into its context. A report could be produced showing where incompatibilities occurred, or in some cases rules, logic and relationships could be implemented so that some adjustments were made to ensure components fitted together in an acceptable way.

Now you know your BIM environment

Having carried out all these audit processes we now know the potential maximum and minimum limits of our BIM environment. The bounds within which a BIM initiative can operate have been established. Initially this audit process will be seen as an overhead on the practice or the project team. Eventually it will become part of accepted procedure because in due course there will be a realisation that going through these audits actually produces cost benefits in the long run and short-circuits many downstream problems and claims. The results of the audits will be interesting and revealing. Keep an eye on your information management and do not let consistency slip.

Post metrics – a convergence plan

Even if the quest for a BIM environment went no further, it would actually have progressed. Why? Because everybody's relevant characteristics of working together are now known. If everyone refused to budge an inch from their positions, the situation could be managed better because the limits have been identified and boundaries of BIM have been established.

Companies with disparate roles and responsibilities or different software platforms, for example, know this and can work accordingly. If there is a variety of 'information standards' then correlations between islands of information can be assembled. Moving away from the minimum position, the assumption would be that the team wanted to improve on bare essentials. Post metrics aspects of BIM that would be priorities for development would be agreed and an implementation programme put in place.

A couple of very straightforward examples follow that incur no cost, require no investment and need no further training or software updates and which are painful in their simplicity of execution and useful to all concerned.

Locating information so that it fits together better

	1	2	3	4	5	6	7
Locating information	Common overall origin	Common origin for each building	Work in the positive quadrant	Use a common grid labelling convention	Relate to OS origin if appropriate	Common orientation	Common setting out

FIGURE 10.12 Locating information.

Take these simple means of locating information in a graphics file. At some stage all team players should establish a universal origin that covers the entirety of the proposed development. Any separate building blocks or phases that are part of the design should share common starting positions. Most systems allow co-ordinates in all four mathematical quadrants, but it makes life easier to keep the site in the positive quadrant just in case anyone has to deal in co-ordinate positions. It is useful to have a common grid and grid labelling system. Some prefer to label A onwards across the top and numbers up or down the side; some alphabetically up or down the side and numbers across. If there is no agreement on how this works, grid references can mean several different positions and lead to chaos. Common orientations and setting out add to the reliability of information fitting together in the most useful way.

In the figures that follow the headings 'Architects', 'M&E Consultants' and 'Structural Engineers' have been used. Any combination of organisational type could have been used; for example, contractor, facility manager, operator, client steel fabricator or cladding manufacturer.

The audit might have revealed the following results:

	1	2	3	4	5	6	7
Locating information	Common overall origin	Common origin for each building	Work in the positive quadrant	Use a common grid labelling convention	Relate to OS origin if appropriate	Common orientation	Common setting out
Architects	✔	✗	✗	✔	✗	✗	✗
M&E Consultants	✗	✔			✔	✗	✗
Structural Engineers	✗	✗	✔	✔	✗	✗	✗

	Non co-operation										Co-operation
Score											
Target											

FIGURE 10.13 A sample 'locating information' audit and target improvement.

The results show a score of six areas where the companies have their own policy on any one of the seven principles. For example, Architects have a policy on using a common origin for everyone engaged on projects in its office. M&E Consultants have a policy of using a common origin for each building block and Structural Engineers have a policy for working in the positive quadrant. The team member agrees, and proves if necessary, that these principles of fitting information together are used on a consistent basis within their practice. They agree to adopt a common convention on principles one to five on the project they are now working on together.

Precision

Information precision	1	2	3	4
	Use the accuracy of snap codes	Work at full size – no scaling	Use accurate dimensions from the model – no eyeballing	Use a common unit of measurement
Architects	✔	✔	✕	✔
M&E Consultants	✕	✔	✔	✕
Structural Engineers	✕	✕	✔	✔

	Non co-operation								Co-operation
Score									
Target									

FIGURE 10.14 A sample 'information precision' audit and target improvement.

In the second set of principles shown above, Architects have a policy that all 2D and 3D graphic construction should only use the accurate snap codes found on all CAD platforms. There should be no 'freehand' input. This assists in ensuring the integrity of all constructed graphics. Architects and M&E Consultants always work at full scale within their graphic databases. M&E Consultants and Structural Engineers have a policy to exclusively use the in-built dimensioning system provided by their CAD platforms. This means that dimensions derived from graphics by the system itself should not be overridden by 'manually' inputting dimensions. Architects and Structural Engineers have policies on using a common unit of measurement, for example millimetres or metres to three decimal places.

Where, who and what?

Information conventions	1 Folder/directory naming conventions	2 File naming conventions	3 File content standards
Architects	✗	✔	✗
M&E Consultants	✗	✔	✔
Structural Engineers	✗	✗	✔

	Non co-operation					Co-operation		
Score								
Target								

FIGURE 10.15 A sample 'information conventions' audit and target improvement.

The 'Where, Who and What?' metric shows that none of the companies have a convention for the way they structure and name folders. Architects and M&E Consultants have file naming conventions,and M&E Consultants and Structural Engineers have a file content standard. At this stage the team have two choices, they may decide to stick with their own approach, but now this audit is public knowledge within the team they could decide to 'map' between their respective conventions. In other words they understand where each is storing different types of information. This simple discovery will, of itself, lead to better information management.

Even if individual practices do not move from their original positions, getting into the habit of carrying out this exercise when they meet a new team means they become more agile at adapting to and utilising the conventions of others. Alternatively if these companies were part of a framework agreement or other form of longer term arrangement they may regard this as the first phase of working towards harmonising their conventions. If teams did this more, commonality might emerge in the form of a de facto standard. The 'target' shows they have decided these options to be suboptimal, so they agree to discard them altogether and go all out to align their conventions.

Things get a little more complicated

The realms of process and workflows, roles and responsibilities is probably one of the most difficult areas in which to get agreement. Often all members of the team will claim to have their own processes and role and responsibility descriptions. Over time office folklore kicks in and things change gradually to a position which is sometimes far removed from the starting point.

Scale as discussed previously comes into play here. Smaller practices may well have their processes and know who does what. For a practice with one or more people who are within easy reach of each other, processes and roles may well be informal. New entrants to the practice are inculcated into how the business operates simply by being there and seeing what goes on and asking questions.

Medium sized practices where people are separated either in different parts of a building or spread across a number of premises, processes and roles will have a degree of formality, perhaps expressed in the form of an office manual. Large scale interdisciplinary companies with several geographical locations will almost certainly have their process and roles manuals; whether people observe them is another question. The 'folklore phenomenon' will make itself felt and over a period of time is likely to transform any formality into the 'we have always done it this way' mantra. It is crucial to medium and large scale practices that they constantly review and update their processes and roles and responsibilities so that they are in as prepared a state as possible to make revisions when deploying a BIM strategy.

In this case all companies claim to have processes in place to plan and programme information. Structural Engineers have processes for checking, approving and changing information. M&E Consultants have processes for assessing information risk (for example the possibility of information not being available on time, scope gaps in information, not enough information). The target is to ensure all companies have processes in place for each category of activity. Analysing existing situations is absolutely fundamental in teasing out processes that are often invisible or unnamed; they are the ones which are taken for granted and can lead to information dysfunction.

This is an area where further drilling down is often required. Questionnaires, interviews, facilitated workshops and more process diagrams may be necessary to establish precisely what processes are in place and whether there is any commonality between the companies or team members. Processes are dissected to explain the overall pattern of work to give a context to specific events where information management does or should occur. It follows that information interfaces and the nature, timing and priority of information to be exchanged can be established. In the end we want BIM to deliver accurate, co-ordinated and timely information to all project team members.

BIM processes	1 Planning information	2 Programming information	3 Review, check and approve information	4 Change implementation	5 Information risk management
Architects	✔	✔	✗	✗	✗
M&E Consultants	✔	✔	✗	✗	✔
Structural Engineers	✔	✔	✔	✔	✗

	Non co-operation											Co-operation
Score												
Target												

FIGURE 10.16 A sample 'BIM processes' audit and target improvement.

Analysing current processes can be frequently underfunded and its real value neglected. If there is a decision to change processes then often there is a temptation to allocate more resources to what is hoped will be the new situation. The main purpose at this stage is to identify disconnects in information supply between individuals and companies so that better value can be attached to information exchange.

If improvements to information management are being considered internally then existing processes will have to be overhauled as part of implementing the targets. This activity begins with the development of an executive consensus as discussed previously in the section dealing with the business case for BIM. Winning hearts and minds is central to the success of the effort. The principle of this managerial commitment applies whatever the scale of practice under consideration.

Having reached this stage there are several broad options facing the companies who have been audited. If it is felt that working in a BIM environment with other team members is likely to be a one-off, then the decision might be simply to fall in with the processes required to support the BIM team on this particular project. If that is the case then there might be minimal process re-engineering required or permitted back at base – a 'we only do enough to get through' sort of mentality. Existing processes would be retained up to the point of participation in BIM.

Alternatively, participating in a BIM environment on a project may be used as a pilot initiative with a view to making changes at base should the concept be proved to some extent. Changing processes is never an easy task; resistance to change is always there so the audit results and a first BIM experience might constitute a first phase of change. A never ending quest for business opportunities might mean that the audit carried out in preparation for BIM participation is used as a catalyst for a more ambitious change. Juggling change in among on-going projects is not an easy thing to achieve.

	1	2	3	4	5	6	7
Roles and responsibilities	Design leader	Lead designer	Project manager	Team manager	Document manager	CAD manager	Contract manager
Architects	✔	✗	✔	✗	✗	✔	✗
M&E Consultants	✗	✗	✗	✔	✔	✔	✗
Structural Engineers	✔	✗	✔	✔	✗	✔	✔

	Non co-operation										Co-operation
Score											
Target											

FIGURE 10.17 A sample 'conventional roles and responsibilities' audit and target improvement.

In this case Architects and M&E Consultants have descriptions for three of these commonly used roles, with Structural Engineers having five. They have decided to be bold and set a target of a common understanding among all three companies for the duration of working together in a BIM environment. The example shows the familiar patchiness of the availability and commonality in roles and responsibilities between Architects, M&E Consultants and Structural Engineers. The purpose of this audit in terms of BIM information is to ascertain:

• Who has responsibility for generating information at different levels and stages?
• Who reviews information and is accountable for its quality and status?

- Who is responsible for the timing of information flows?
- Who is responsible for notifying others as to its availability and time of arrival?

What might be

The next two metrics shown on roles and process are hypothetical. They are specifically aimed towards BIM management as opposed to the metrics described above, which have simply taken a cross section of commonly used terms from current practice and which can be converted into a BIM context.

Defining BIM Processes

BIM process control	1 BIM strategic planning	2 BIM development and implementation	3 BIM programme management	4 BIM information preparation and review	5 BIM input	6 BIM change	7 BIM focusing/ discipline	8 BIM information risk management
Architects								
M&E Consultants								
Structural Engineers								

FIGURE 10.18 Hypothetical process audit template for a BIM environment.

1 BIM strategic planning

Strategic planning of the BIM should begin by instigating a series of audits based on those discussed earlier. The outcome should shape the extent of a common understanding of what the BIM environment will look like. The principles are the same for any scale of company or team; use should be made of what is appropriate in any given context.

- Would it cover the entire project life cycle or some sub-set of it?
- Which collection of software should be used and what is its information exchange performance?
- What sort of information is manufactured by individual authors – 2D, 3D, objects and to what degree, or parametrics?
- Which conventions should be adopted for structuring information?

- Is the BIM environment voluntary or backed up by procurement, contractual or employment documentation?

2 BIM development and implementation

Once the scene is set, then comes the task of ensuring it becomes a reality.

- Where is the BIM to be located? – office server, remote server, web portal, server farm?
- Test communications – wifi communications, intranet, extranet and web connections.
- Test the chosen software collection and its ability to connect together where necessary.
- Create shared and focus/discipline group areas.
- Create the information structure for folders and file contents, including any standard templates.
- Ensure all members have access to the BIM environment.
- Monitor the performance of the BIM over time.

3 BIM programme management

BIM programme management in this context means the timing of inputs, outputs and updates to the BIM. Clearly information cannot just come and go as anyone pleases in the BIM environment, given this is a collaborative atmosphere where everyone working in a small office or a larger manifestation of BIM has access to BIM information which is open, editable and shared. It would be possible for anyone to 'chip in' at any time but this would most likely lead to chaos. Nevertheless contributions must be made to the shared information environment, but in an orderly fashion.

A programme of when it is appropriate to make interventions to the BIM must be formulated and this will have to be co-ordinated with the normal design and construction programmes. This is one of the responsibilities of the BIM Manager.

4 BIM information preparation and review

Disciplines or focus groups will prepare their own information, for example design concepts, structural concepts and general arrangements in their own area of the BIM. That might physically be on their computers in a small office implementation of BIM, or on their own computers but connected to an intranet which has a route out to a private area on a remote server in larger implementations of BIM.

Once an individual or group feels information is ready they should ensure it is checked and peer reviewed internally before submitting it to the BIM. This will entail making sure any new or amended information is properly co-ordinated with the latest version extracted from the

BIM. Information should be audited to ensure it conforms to the agreed BIM conventions and only the absolutely necessary information is ready for entry to the shared BIM environment.

Pre-preparation also implies assessing whether there will be any consequential effect on other interested parties, for example does the new information impact on overall programmes or resource levels? Pre-preparation reviews may take place at a number of levels depending on whether the information being produced has an impact on detailed design or overall project strategy. The BIM Manager may set out a programme for routine reviews and their approval sought for any other specific checkups. The BIM Author or the BIM Focus Group/Discipline Manager should be the point of contact for the pre-preparation process.

5 BIM input

When an information author is confident that all quality control processes are complete then information can make its entry into the shared domain. Existing information must be carefully removed and the new integrated with precision. All interested parties should be informed of the latest amendments, and any anomalies reconciled because although localised checking will ensure the new information batch is consistent within itself, its integration might reveal further co-ordination is necessary.

Although all information will be tagged to show who the author was, its ownership is now in the collective possession of the BIM players. The BIM Manager should then inform everyone that is the case. The BIM Manager should also inform BIM members about any change in status; in other words, is the new version for information only, for comment, draft, final, or capable of being acted upon, for example?

6 BIM change

As we all know change can come at us from all directions and involve minor or major adjustments to any aspect of a project. It should be established when and by whom change can be instigated, as well as at what level and which processes. Change of another sort might be necessary. The original information structuring conventions require attention over time. The BIM Manager along with the BIM Technologist should ensure that information conforms to the norm. However as the BIM environment develops extensions to the BIM information structure will inevitably be required. The information structure should not be allowed to grow like Topsy; ad hoc modifications and inventions to information structuring techniques should be outlawed otherwise information will become a liability with severe consequences.

New requirements should be carefully thought out and presented by BIM Authors. Consensus on new areas of conventions should be reached and a phased implementation plan made.

7 BIM focusing/discipline

The focusing/discipline process focuses on how the BIM should be compartmentalised to deal with issues, for example zoning or phasing a development, partial or sequential completion or the integration of the work of various disciplines. Focusing will be dynamic in that input will be required from different groups of project team players according to priorities.

8 BIM information risk management

The nature of risk to information in the BIM environment must be thought through. What constitutes risk to information? There are the technological issues of losing information by any cause, for example servers going down, communications links failing, information corruption, viruses and hacking. Some of these are new to our way of working but the future will see more and more tampering with information by mischief or commercial sabotage as it journeys around the virtual world.

Then there are what might be termed the normal types of risk with information: Is it late? Is it too much or too little? Is it wrong or inadequate? Has it been checked properly? Is it the information the next person wants? Is it clear? Has it been structured wrongly?

The BIM therefore requires its own risk register which will follow the normal format of risk identification, ownership, impact assessment, mitigation and prevention. Following normal practice the risk register should be reviewed at regular intervals.

Defining BIM roles – small and large office

Scale plays its part in which roles might occur. In a small office, as always, people tend to be something of a jack of all trades. Various roles described below may reside with one or two people only. It would not be unthinkable to envisage a situation where the roles of BIM Manager, BIM Technologist and the BIM Author were fulfilled by one and the same person in a small to medium sized practice. Currently a partner or director in a mainstream practice might struggle to combine the roles of BIM Director and BIM Manager.

In contrast, BIM on a large scale project may have people in post to cover all the roles discussed above. Indeed some roles may necessitate one or more people. The BIM Technologist role, for example, might consist of a person whose expertise lies in web technologies, whereas another may be an expert on a particular software platform.

The BIM may be quite complex and long term in which case the BIM Manager might have assistants or deputies who are responsible for certain sections of the BIM. Perhaps architecture and construction is waiting for a new breed of person who is able to take on the mantle of BIM Director. There are few people who can combine business, project and technological expertise to ensure the successful stewardship of a major BIM initiative.

	1	2	3	4	5	6	7
BIM roles and responsibilities	BIM Director	BIM Manager	BIM Focus/ Discipline Group Manager	BIM Author	BIM Technologist	BIM Support	BIM HR Manager
Architects							
M&E Consultants							
Structural Engineers							

FIGURE 10.19 Hypothetical roles and responsibilities audit template for a BIM environment.

BIM Director

The BIM Director has overall responsibility for the strategic formulation and implementation of the BIM throughout the life cycle of the BIM. In a conventional design and construct life cycle the BIM Director would be one person appointed for the duration of the project. Where there is a long term large scale property portfolio, for example hospitals, universities or infrastructure, and where the cycle of design, construct, use and recycle is never ending, the BIM Directorship may be handed to someone with the relevant expertise for any given stage.

BIM Manager

The BIM Manager has overall day-to-day responsibility for operating the BIM:

- interfacing with the project team
- information flows and quality
- the short and long term security of information
- training, software and information structuring conventions
- support
- human resources.

BIM Focus/Discipline Group Manager

From time to time different constituencies within the BIM environment will be the front runners in generating information for a specific purpose or timescale. The BIM Focus/ Discipline Group Manager is a dynamic role for a person or practice who might lead that team temporarily until focus shifts to a different group. At any stage the focus may be on a particular phase, a certain portion of the project, a planning issue, HVAC co-ordination, asset inventory or energy use, for example. In which case, managing information may be better handled by a specialist for that purpose in the interim.

BIM Author

A BIM Author is any individual or company who creates information for the BIM environment. Their contribution would, of course, be dictated by the role their conventional area of expertise plays in the immediate or extended team and supply chain. Their input would be governed by the targets agreed based on the outcome of the various audits. In an ideal world this way of working would be adopted on a voluntary basis, but could be reinforced by making stipulations in procurement documents and added as a project protocol to the JCT Constructing Excellence (CE) form of contract, for example.

BIM Technologist

The BIM Technologist is responsible for managing all aspects of software, hardware and communications. This is a wide remit in today's world. An important activity within the scope of this role would be to carefully evaluate the findings of the software and versions audit to ensure that the technology 'fits together' with the least disruption to all concerned. BIM will increasingly operate in a virtual world as pressure increases to move information around rather than people, so the BIM Technologist will have to keep abreast of a wide range of new and emerging technologies.

BIM Support

This role would be the trouble-shooter in the BIM environment, working with every other role in the team to ensure things run smoothly. In particular BIM Support would provide initial assistance to the core project team as it formed and then further afield to the extended core team and to any supply chain members who are part of the BIM environment. BIM focus groups may need support because of their temporary nature, depending on the expertise of the nominated manager.

BIM HR Manager

The BIM HR Manager is vitally important. This role ensures the best expertise with the correct attitude is provided within the BIM environment. The BIM HR Manager can perform audits on practices and groups if existing personnel are to form the BIM project team or the BIM HR Manager can be responsible for recruiting appropriate know-how. The BIM HR Manager requires a thorough understanding of the skills and techniques involved in BIM and should also be able to have specialist expertise in being able to screen people for their attitudes towards collaborative working.

AIA Document E202–2008 (AIA 2008)

This document from the American Institute of Architects was mentioned earlier. It is instructive and is one of the few practical documents that mainstream practice could pick up and use as a guide with little financial outlay. It is far more palatable than some of the technical material that is currently extant. The full title is *AIA Document E202–2008, Building Information Modeling Protocol Exhibit* (BIM-PE) and it is available from the AIA web site.

There are several notable items at the beginning of the document. The first is that it is in the form of a legal agreement. There are places at the head of the BIM-PE for parties to enter the normal details, name, address and so on that would appear on any standard form of contract. Next, it provides a formal basis for committing parties to a BIM environment by stating that the BIM-PE will be annexed to another agreement, the details of which have to be given. Presumably in the American context this would be appended to a standard Design Bid Build or Design Build contract.

In the UK it would now be possible and more in keeping with Egan and Latham exhortations to append such a thing to a far more collaborative form of contract such as the JCT CE contract, the Strategic Forum for Construction's Integrated Project Team agreement or NEC3.

The final and most striking declaration is 'This document has important legal consequences. Consultation with an attorney is encouraged with respect to its completion or modification.' Unfortunately, whilst representing a step forward in terms of giving a big boost to the use of BIM methodology, the mood of the document resides in a traditional adversarial world. The BIM-PE then has an initial section on definitions of terms used within the agreement. What BIM means in this context is 'a digital representation of the physical and functional characteristics of the Project'; a very loose interpretation of BIM. There then follow three definitions which are central to the whole thesis behind the BIM-PE; 'Level Of Development' (LOD), 'Model Element' and 'Model Element Author'.

A checklist of elements similar to the ones which appear in *The Architects' Journal* for cost analysis or the BCIS elemental cost structure is used as a framework to define who is going to provide information about each element and the LOD determines to what extent. The definitions also tell us that the Model Element Author is responsible for providing BIM content to the specified level, and any discrepancies with the model should be notified to its author immediately. Normal copyright on model content applies.

Further 'clauses' govern the following:

- Managing the model, assumed to be the architect unless otherwise stated.
- Responsibilities for defining model conventions, for example model origin, storage structure, input and output processes, access rights.
- Management of the integration of incoming models.
- Management of clash detection and their resolution.
- Management of archive material.

The next section specifies requirements for the LOD and it identifies five levels which can be used in successive degrees of detail. The first refers to what might be called massing, a level of information where information is provided that is suitable for geometric estimates, approximate cost analyses and scheduling of results. In all five levels there is provision to add other 'authorised uses', presumably with agreement between the BIM contributors.

The second covers the same ground except 'non-geometric information' could be included, analyses are supplemented by 'generalized criteria assigned to model elements', and costing carried out by 'conceptual estimating techniques'. Schedules may be used to indicate the inclusion of elements over time. Level three specifies that 'Model Elements are modeled as specific assemblies accurate in terms of quantity, size, shape, location, and orientation. Non-geometric information may also be attached to Model Elements.' Again, schedules may be used to indicate the inclusion of elements over time. Level four is as above plus 'complete fabrication, assembly, and detailing information such that the model is suitable for construction', proper performance can be analysed, costs are actual and 'the model can be used to show time-scale appearance of specific elements and systems including construction means and methods'. Level five is 'as constructed' information.

Article four declares that each model author's content is to be shared with other authors throughout the project. If an author provides information above the LOD then other authors are advised to rely on it only to the extent of the LOD and the next part of the document provides cover indemnity should they do so. This is just a brief description of some of the content of the AIA's document but several important points can be drawn from its tentative entry into the legalistic arena. At the time of writing there is nothing like this in the UK published by the professional architecture and construction institutions. If anything exists it is due to the pragmatic approach adopted by any companies who seek to legislate for BIM.

The document shows one of the first attempts to marry IT, BIM in this case, with a legal framework. The declaration at the start advising consultation with an attorney is a typical litigious standpoint displayed in the USA. It would have been better to eliminate the statement, which would have immediately affected the mood of the document; more collaborative language could have been used. This is not a lengthy document, some nine pages long, and therefore its attempt to legislate for everyone and every type of information that might be part of a project is limited and begs many questions, for example: What type of geometry – solids or extrusions? What kind of non-graphic data? How much fabrication, assembly and detailing information? What are satisfactory 'Levels Of Development' for specific elements?

In future the AIA Document E208 could be developed to include parametric objects. If so, the extent to which they displayed behaviour and relationships would require further definition of original authors, subsequent authors and virtual authors as well as the indemnification which might be involved. Given the ascendency of BIM it is only a matter of time before more and more cases appear in the Technology and Construction Court based on BIM itself and which fall outside conventional claims under contract or tort. Will documents such as this inhibit or encourage a new breed of claim? There is no doubt that it blazes a trail; only time will tell.

▶ **SUMMARY**

How do we implement BIM?

- Remember a BIM strategy is a business strategy.

- BIM must have executive backing.

- Identifying the BIM mindset is crucial.

- BIM implementation principles apply to any scale of business.

- Apply the metrics rigorously.

- Choose realistic targets.

- Implement as much or as little as is comfortable – overambition will lead to failure.

- Phase the integration of BIM into the business.

- Keep abreast of technology trends and innovations.

- Use the sample metrics to establish where the team stands in terms of collaboration.

SECTION 11
BIM in a collaborative legal context

Islands of contract

BIM as a means of co-operating through information management in the project team is currently at odds with the legal and commercial environment in which it has been invented and hopefully develops. Contracts and procurement documentation tend to insulate and isolate rather than collaborate. They set boundaries and barriers which are not conducive to working in a BIM mode.

In the 70s and 80s a common concept in the CAD world was one of islands of information. Every CAD platform generated its information and at one time in CAD history it was very difficult to move information from one platform to another. At first it was thought that special translators would have to be devised for each pair of software platforms that wanted to communicate. Information was stranded on its originating platform with little prospect of going anywhere else. Standard means of information exchange came into use and gradually the islands became connected; still to this day, not ideally.

Legal commercial arrangements are similar to this. One contract tends to define one pair of relationships or one set of requirements in a project, each having little regard for the other. Documents prepare for attack and defence, talking in terms of errors, omissions, shall, will and other words and phrases that mean every project team player is wary of another. Copyright and intellectual property provisions in agreements are an implicit form of ring-fencing information. A single island is a single interest and that is unlikely to be in the project's interest as well as in the collective interest of the entire team. We must reconcile these opposing stances if BIM is to flourish, otherwise there will always be a tension between commercial arrangement and BIM operation.

Collaborative contracts

The NEC3, ACA2000, the Strategic Forum for Contruction's Integrated Project Team (IPT) agreement and JCT Constructing Excellence (CE) forms of contract were steps towards a more positive world. The IPT agreement states:

The Partners and Cluster Partners undertake not to make any claim against each other for any loss or damage whatsoever arising out of or in connection with this Agreement, including claims arising out of prior discussions, claims alleging negligence and claims for injunctive relief.

and the JCT CE contract states:

The Overriding Principle guiding the Purchaser and the Supplier in the operation of this Contract is that of collaboration. It is their intention to work together with each other and with all other Project Participants in a co-operative and collaborative manner in good faith and in the spirit of mutual trust and respect. To this end the Purchaser and the Supplier agree they shall each give to, and welcome from, the other, and the other Project Participants, feedback on performance and shall draw each other's attention to any difficulties and shall share information openly, at the earliest practicable time. They shall support collaborative behaviour and address behaviour that does not comply with the Overriding Principle.

These are radically different and very powerful statements made early on in the text of the contracts. They present a valuable variation on the long tradition of adversarialism that has been extant in forms of contract hitherto. The 'Overriding Principle' is not a sentimental aspiration but something that has the backing of the courts in the form of Rule 1.1 of the Civil Procedure Rules supplied by the Ministry of Justice.

Guidance to the rule indicates that the 'Overriding Principle' takes precedence over any other clause in the contract, thereby affording it an incontrovertible superiority. If interpretation or dispute resolution is required then it will be done in the best interests of the Overriding Principle. In other words those who can demonstrate the closest adherence to the Overriding Principle win the day.

The Rules ensure:

- Cases are dealt with in a just manner.
- The parties are equal under the Overriding Principle.
- The parties should have least cost.
- Proportionality of value, importance and complexity.

Parties signing this type of agreement are making a serious commitment to working together. Both forms ask the participants to sign up to a declaration of mutual trust and support; they must co-operate as much as possible and blame as little as possible. This is something of an anathema to many project teams and design and build contractors.

However, in a legal framework such as this, BIM can blossom and the real advantages of managing information electronically can be realised. Following on from the Overriding Principle both forms include several key notions. The agreements assume the project team will act as one. In the extreme a single company might be formed where all members are in effect stakeholders in the project. The client of course is one of the main players in this scenario and it is crucial that they are a signatory to the collaborative cause. Perhaps the client has to accept more of a position as 'one of the team' and less one of the piper calling the tune. After all it is the team who convert the client's money into long term value, a symbiotic relationship.

The idea of a single entity would be reinforced by having one lawyer as part of the team. The lawyer's role would be to ensure fair play and interpret situations to the benefit of the team using the Overriding Principle as their scales of justice. Both forms of contract provide for a Board, part of whose role is to act as an 'internal court' with the intention of resolving issues before traditional litigation routes are followed. The lawyer could perhaps chair this board on appropriate occasions. The single entity idea then begs the question of single project insurance. This tends to go hand in hand with another concept common to be agreements and that is a notion of a joint responsibility for pain and gain. The idea behind the pain/gain share is to accept that things do go wrong, the unexpected happens on projects. People do make mistakes; information can be incorrect on occasions. When this occurs the predominant consequence is almost certainly financial.

A full explanation of the pain/gain share is not the focus of this book. However, a working concept might be helpful. Identifying the pain/gain share relies heavily on more open forms of project accounting as well as creating and effectively managing a risk register. Each party declares the basic labour and material cost of doing the job as a target, they also show their overhead and profit component. In addition the entire group as it evolves assesses components of risk both for themselves and for any groupings (co-ordination by structural engineer or HVAC engineer suspended ceiling supplier, for example) that might occur. The cash consequence of the aggregate of all these risk items is the amount insured against, in other words project insurance. Ideally this leads to a situation where profit and overhead are ring-fenced as are the consequences of things going wrong. If actual costs exceed or come below the target for constituent parts of the overall cost, then the pain or gain is shared in a proportion agreed by the parties to that particular aspect of the job at the outset. Given the profound influence of the Overriding Principle, eliminating risk by insurance, almost guaranteeing profit and overhead, and an incentive to preserve 'gain' should, in theory at any rate, give the project team a more comfortable environment in which to work. The insurer would be part of the team and could perhaps work alongside the lawyer to ensure fair play.

Technology can only make BIM work to a limited extent. The commercial arrangements which form the background and create the mood of the team are, at the very least, equally important. These new forms of agreement, and that is a better word than contract, are not perfect and they are in their infancy. It is something of a contradiction in terms to say there is little, if anything, in terms of case law to show whether they have major flaws or can be exploited in a way that was not intended.

▶ SUMMARY
BIM in a collaborative legal context
• The legal landscape in which BIM operates must change.
• Traditional legal arrangements tend to create barriers and isolationism.
• New forms of collaborative contract offer a different legal backdrop.
• The 'Overriding Principle' points the way to a new set of values for the project team.
• Is the pain/gain share a new way forward?
• Can there be just one lawyer and one insurer in a project team?

SECTION 12
BIM as an agent for cultural change

Social technology compared with architectural and construction technology

BIM viewed through technological eyes may appear to have had a limited effect on cultural change in architecture and construction, and yet interactions with architectural and construction technology can have severe consequences when things go wrong. The technology has simply quickened communications and design team interactions. The litigiosity and adversarial nature of the interactions has not changed at all. Indeed some would say that technology has simply served to speed up the process of reaching the point at which claims and litigation to create profit margin can be attained.

Currently, the collection of software platforms commonly used for BIM encourage compartmentalisation of design activity and information storage due to commercial drivers. Providing seamless information management outside the domain of an individual software vendor is not a sales-attractive proposition either for vendor or purchaser at the moment. As a consequence they tend to reinforce legal separatism and therefore hinder design and construction interaction rather than support it. Let us hope this situation changes and the importance of information manager becomes a high priority once the benefits are appreciated. It is unlikely this will happen in any significant way until the nature of architectural and construction interactions change and the role of information within that context is seen as an agent for collaboration rather than a Cinderella subject.

In an ideal world a new generation of software is called for, one that knows no commercial, vendor or technical boundaries and that produces and maintains information in a single consistent way. This is very unlikely to happen of course. However, some examples such as the Open Source Initiative develops software to educate about, and advocate for, the benefits of open source and to build bridges among different constituencies in the open-source community. One of the most important activities as a standards body is to maintain the Open Source Definition for the good of the community. The Open Source Initiative Approved License trademark and programme creates a nexus of trust around which developers, users, corporations and governments can organise open-source co-operation.

These are powerful statements of intent and have no equivalent in the architecture and construction software developer and user fraternity. The development of the Unix operating system which grew out of the use of early DEC computers by the people at Bell Laboratories is a similar story. In other business sectors some global players such as Proctor & Gamble or Goldcorp, a Canadian gold mining firm, have placed a substantial amount of their intellectual property in the public domain on the web in the hope that a global web community would see ways of using it they had not. Their bold step, which runs counter to a protectionist view of information, proved to be successful and many new opportunities were discovered.

The web has created new spaces for interaction with clear advantage, but the idea has not made its appearance in the mercantile world of architecture and construction as it has for social web spaces. The crux of the matter lies in the search for a different commercial basis for collaboration in architecture and construction before existing technology can play its part more effectively. However, it is possible that should a new significant commercial basis emerge, then current software may prove to be irrelevant or obsolete.

▶ **SUMMARY**

BIM as an agent for cultural change

- BIM struggles to have a cultural impact.
- Cultural change is not as simple as the changes brought about by social technology.

SECTION 13
Government BIM

Launch of a nationwide initiative

What followed Paul Morrell's initial declarations on BIM has been one of the most profound initiatives for change in the construction industry in modern times. The Government through its BIM Task Group instigated a UK wide programme to change the way the Government property portfolio is procured. In future, procurement should focus on reducing costs in capital expenditure and delivering a valuable information asset that will target operating expenditure in a more efficient way. It launched a series of so-called BIM Regional Hubs throughout England, Scotland, Wales and Northern Ireland which provide a regional focal point for anyone connected with the construction industry to get involved with the initiative.

At the same time the central Task Group worked with Government on a number of pilot projects which were aimed at illustrating the benefits of BIM working and which began to embed BIM processes at the heart of Government departmental procurement.

This initiative has generated the widest possible support and interest in the industry, from all professions, trades, supply chain members, product manufacturers, the legal profession and regulatory bodies.

A 180-cell extension to Cookham Wood prison in Kent procured in 2012 on behalf of the Ministry of Justice was the first pilot for the use of BIM methodologies on Government projects.

There was felt to be enough benefit from introducing BIM in terms of cost benefit, and a willingness on the part of suppliers to engage, that the Ministry of Justice issued notice that a further three projects would be put out to tender on the basis that BIM is to be used.

The importance of the 28 February 2013 documents (PAS 1192, COBie, CIC BIM Protocol, RIBA Plan of Work 2013)

The first two or three years of the BIM initiative culminated in 2013 with the publication of several documents, which symbolise the ethic of the initiative while at the same time providing the industry with the framework in which to implement BIM.

In many respects the documents consolidate what was out there in the first place but, because they are issued as part of this Government BIM procurement programme, they are provoking a radical reappraisal of working practices within the industry.

At the heart of the BIM initiative is the idea of more co-operation between those who produce the Government's property stock, whether it be buildings or infrastructure.

The documents and the initiative have provoked a change in mood. Many involved have breathed a sigh of relief that, at last, there might be a better way of working on the horizon, one that reduces adversarialism, waste and inefficiency with benefit for all construction stakeholders.

Whether individuals and organisations are involved with Government procurement cycles or not the initiative has awakened a feeling that there is a form of better practice if the principles contained in the documents are adopted.

PAS 1192 Demystified

While having a rather forbidding and unprepossessing title this document probably represents the most significant of the 28 February 2013 BIM Task Group publications.

The acronym PAS stands for Publicly Available Specification which means it is a consultative document produced by an organisation that wants to standardise best practice on a specific subject. A full British Standard has reached entire consensus, whereas a PAS invites comments but need not incorporate them, thus minimising the time taken to reach a majority opinion, although not necessarily an absolute opinion.

PAS 1192 sets out processes and standards that provide a good practice framework for more co-operative working by project teams supported by IT. It makes use of what is out there already but places emphasis on using software and standards in an atmosphere of mutual trust and understanding. In the past project teams have tended to work in islands of isolation whereas PAS 1192 advocates using what has traditionally been used in terms of software, process and standards, but with more communication between project team members and more understanding of what they are using and trying to achieve with their information.

A key aim of the document is to create a new and more valuable information asset for the client, whether public or private, for use throughout project life cycle.

PAS 1192 outlines what has now become a landmark expression in the world of the Government BIM initiative: 'BIM Level 2 readiness'. This is a state of operation that the industry should aim to reach by 2016 to achieve the Government's target.

Level 2 readiness means:

- Having a clear and English language idea of what the client's information requirements are at every stage of a project. Knowing your information marketplace.
- Being clear about the roles and responsibilities of everyone concerned with producing information for the project.
- Having a clear plan for delivering structured and quality controlled information.
- Having a clear view of how project software platforms interact.

Prior to contracts being awarded, PAS 1192 gives guidance on what project teams should have in place when tendering for jobs to demonstrate they are 'BIM ready'. This includes:

- A clear view of the client's information requirements at each stage and its ultimate strategic use.
- Any BIM training which the immediate project team or entire supply chain might need.
- Conformance to BS 1192 in terms of origin locations, file naming and other information structuring conventions.
- A schedule of software, their versions and their information exchange capabilities.
- Discipline responsibilities and work package content.
- Methods of information co-ordination and clash detection.

PAS 1192 asks each member of the project team to supply a BIM Execution Plan (BEP) which indicates how information will be produced and managed, and gives an assessment, pre-contract of each member's BIM credentials – resources, IT and previous BIM jobs, if any.

Post contract, PAS 1192 asks for confirmation of reliable and timely information delivery, standards, resource availability, IT platforms and training needs.

Each project team and supply chain member should contribute their own information delivery plan to a master delivery plan. If all goes well, the overall plan is made available to everyone; IT upgrades and training programmes are then acquired and implemented.

A model consisting of graphic and non-graphic information is gradually developed according to strict quality control processes and ultimately delivered to the client.

There is a certain vocabulary and a set of acronyms used within the document which take a little time to come to terms with, for example: MIDP – Master Information Delivery Plan, CPIx Construction Project Information Xchange. They are perhaps more familiar to some of the bigger contracting organisations or have been invented anew within the BIM context. They may be less useful for the vast majority of SMEs, who constitute a large proportion of the supply chain, and could act as a disincentive for adoption. When they have been understood, most people will recognise them as familiar information management concepts for which they will already have their own and more comfortable terminology.

COBie demystified

COBie is an American import and gives us yet another acronym to contend with; it stands for Construction Operations Building Information Exchange. NASA and the White House Office of Science provided initial funding to establish the requirements of information exchange throughout project life cycle. Its subsequent uptake and development has been given impetus by the General Services Administration and the Corps of Engineers.

In essence COBie's ultimate aim is to a build up every conceivable item of information about any facility throughout its entire life. It starts with the details of all the people and companies involved and overall descriptions of the facility, its floors, geometry and spaces. This roughly equates to the planning and conceptual design stages of a project.

Information accumulation continues through what might be a notional detailed design stage where information about the systems, such as air conditioning or fire protection, is brought into play.

On from there COBie asks for much more detail about assemblies of components or individual components. Finally, comes the information required for facilities management, operation, demolition and recycling. The COBie requirement here goes into very fine detail, for example model number, warranty details, expected life and replacement costs.

A Microsoft Office Excel spreadsheet has been chosen as the medium for storing this information. This has led to some initial difficulties for those who have experimented with COBie. Even if a relatively small facility is involved, this can lead to an extremely large number of rows in the spreadsheet, and large projects have been known to overload Excel's capacity.

As with PAS 1192 some of the terminology is strange both in terms of what it means and in its depiction on the standard spreadsheet headings, for example ExternalSystem, ExternalObject, the latter referring to what many regard as the obscure Ifc exchange format.

But as with PAS 1192, looking beyond the peculiarities then COBie is simply the information that we are all familiar with.

Both in the Government context and in that of general best practice the COBie database is intended to be used at particular work stages in various forms of plans of work to supply what have become known as 'data drops'.

How the information reaches the spreadsheet is 'up for grabs' at the moment. Some software vendors have provided an output channel from their platform; some larger companies can afford to have their 'geeks' manufacture a software interface between their platform and Excel. Some SMEs have had to 'build' the spreadsheet manually. They fall into the trap of regarding the exercise as something that can be done by an office administrator or junior, because 'it is a mundane information copy and paste task'. This usually destroys the information as an asset because inexperienced people do not recognise mistakes in the information or they have no interest in maintaining its integrity. The valuable information asset is lost.

The modest virtues of COBie at the moment are twofold. First the official line is that it is the lowest common denominator database; almost everyone has a copy of Excel and can use it.

The second and more important virtue is that it can help product manufacturers to get their offering locked into the contractor's, lead designer's or employer's models. This is discussed more elsewhere in the book.

BIM Protocol demystified

The Construction Industry Council (CIC) BIM Protocol 'identifies the Building Information Models that are required to be produced by members of the project team and puts into place specific obligations, liabilities and associated limitations on the use of the models'.

The BIM Protocol has several well intentioned aims to assist the project team when it embarks on a BIM project, namely to:

- Support the production of information at defined stages in a plan of work.
- Support project teams in collaborative working in combination with PAS 1192.
- Ensure all team members including members of the supply chain have a BIM protocol as part of their contractual relationships.
- Work alongside common forms of contract.
- Support Level 2 working.
- Offer clarification on the intellectual property of the various parties.
- Offer clarification of the role of the Information Manager.

Most of these are common sense aims which any well organised and professionally managed project team would implement. Two of the aims are worthy of specific comment.

The first is intellectual property (IP). The advent of BIM has generated a discussion on how IP rights might be changed because of BIM working. The BIM Protocol does no more than reaffirm the status quo in that each team member keeps their own IP but grants each other a licence to use their information for the purposes of the project unless legislated otherwise in contractual agreements.

The second point is clarification of the role of the Information Manager. This too has been a source of debate. The Protocol defines this as a separate activity. The Information Manager is responsible for 'the establishment and management of the processes, protocols and procedures set out in the Information Requirements', in other words the way in which models of all varieties are produced, handed over and utilised on the project in conformance with the required standards, methods and procedures.

The significant point is that it is a separate role with no design co-ordination obligation.

Confusion arises because this role could be a completely new breed of person or it could be undertaken by the lead designer, contractor or any other nominated project team member. Whoever it is it would mean a dual obligation of managing the structure and workings of the BIM environment as well as their conventional legal responsibilities.

The BIM Protocol is more of a legal agreement rather than a protocol along the lines of the AIA's E202–2008 document mentioned elsewhere in the book. In this respect it is rather disappointing in that it invents another layer of legality rather than eliminating legal implications and adding support to information management.

All members of the project team are required to have a BIM protocol appended to their contracts. It attempts to ensure everyone has the same information standards in the models they produce on the project.

The BIM Protocol's Appendices get to the heart of what a BIM protocol should be but are sparse in terms of guidance, to say the least. Project teams will have to allow considerable resource to discuss and complete this section of the protocol.

The Specimen Model Production and Delivery Table appears to place the contractor at the centre of the majority of deliverables. Other professions and members of supply chains who may play a critical role are shown as having minor input.

Appendix 2, which could provide more of a stimulus towards convergence on the proposition of a national standard, only indicates skeletal headings.

Overall the emphasis seems to be to the advantage of the contractor. Strategies, policies and assumptions which form the critical feasibility and starting point for any project plus the design stage itself are given minimal status which is a shame since these are the stages when the professions create the lasting value and consequences for any built facility.

The RIBA Plan of Work 2013

The RIBA Plan of Work 2013 is a breath of fresh air as far as BIM is concerned. It is strange how 'the Plan of Work' attracts adverse criticism but is nevertheless the plan that most people and professions refer to, emulate or rewrite. It does seem to be a gold standard within the profession and the construction industry.

The first important strategic point to make is that it is the first RIBA Plan of Work to mention BIM. This represents a seismic shift in perception of what architects must get involved with for the benefit of both themselves and their clients.

Stage 0 does not mention BIM explicitly, but the 'Strategic Brief' appears in the 'Information Exchanges' task bar. The Strategic Brief's formulation contains the assumptions and policies forming the background to the creation of a project whatever shape that project takes. This information may be an important point of reference in downstream design, construction and operation activity.

It is in Stage 1 where the idea of BIM is first introduced explicitly, but briefly, in the context of information exchanges and assembling the team early on.

In many respects this is all that is needed because the 2013 version of the Plan of Work maps to the 2007 version, which is supported by the 2012 BIM Overlay to the RIBA Outline Plan of Work. Presumably the next version of the BIM Overlay will mesh directly with the 2013 version of the Plan of Work.

FIGURE 13.1 Relationship between the RIBA Plans of Work and the BIM Overlay to the RIBA Outline Plan of Work.

The RIBA publication *Assembling a Collaborative Project Team* forms an essential sister document to the RIBA Plan of Work 2013. Assembling the collaborative team and its BIM capability should be achieved as early as possible, at Stage 0 or perhaps even earlier. The Information Exchanges task bar underlines the strategic significance of BIM as the 'Building Information Movement' as discussed elsewhere in the book. It is both a symbolic reminder of how the profession needs to focus more on the information a project team creates on behalf of its client, as well as offering a practical connection to the BIM Overlay as to what information should be shared at each stage.

The UK Government Information Exchanges task bar gives those practices involved in Government procurement cycles a signal that they will ultimately have to take the Soft Landings initiative into account.

The RIBA Plan of Work 2013 offers a far more palatable body of advice and recommendations for the vast majority of SME architectural practices than what might be regarded as a counterpart, PAS 1192. It could be thought of as a 'translation' of PAS 1192 into the world of the SME. Its vocabulary and scale is far more appropriate to mainstream practice and the types of projects they undertake.

The BIM Regional Hubs and special interest groups

The BIM Task Group launched BIM Regional Hubs throughout England, Scotland, Wales and Northern Ireland. The Hubs attracted an extremely wide crosssection of public and private organisations, professions and trades across the entire spectrum of the construction industry.

The obvious candidates, such as MEP engineers, structural engineers, architects and contractors, attended the launch session. What was more encouraging was the presence of solicitors, barristers, environmental consultants, product manufacturers, facilities managers, local authority and regulatory body representatives and emergency services personnel. Anyone involved in the mainstream or any corner of the construction industry could get involved with their local Hub.

The Hubs have several aims

The most important is to act as a conduit between its members and the BIM Task Group. Hubs provide the basis for a dialogue about the overall Government BIM strategy. They represent a forum for the industry to inform the future development of BIM. It is a golden opportunity for everyone to work co-operatively towards a better UK Construction Plc and gain benefit for everyone involved.

Each Hub should have a plan for its development in terms of recruitment and a programme of events. Via these means Hubs should expand. Some of the original Hubs, such as the South East, covered such a vast area that they have spawned smaller county Hubs.

The Hubs attract people with a wide range of BIM expertise. Some believe that the BIM expertise in their organisation is well developed, other brave people admit their understanding of BIM is minimal, although they are usually surprised to find they have been 'doing BIM' already.

Another important function of the Hubs is to bring these people together. People from any corner of the construction industry can join a Hub simply by responding to CIC and Hub publications about future events and meetings. These can be seen on the CIC web site and the Regional Hubs' own web sites and there is now a growing set of LinkedIn communities which show discussions and events. Anyone can pitch in wherever they feel comfortable.

What can members contribute to the Hub or what support can the Hub provide? An important function of the Hubs is to cross-fertilise expertise. There are people and organisations who believe they have started their BIM journey and have valuable experience to pass onto others. The flip side is there are many who are BIM beginners and feel they need to hear the experiences of those who have already put some form of BIM in place.

The Regional Hub Map on the BIM Task Group web site shows twelve Hubs. Some of these already have 'sub Hubs'; for example, Wales has north and south, and the South East Hub has created an Oxford Hub thanks to some young enthusiasts; and there are others to follow.

Apart from the Regional Hubs a series of special interest groups have been created.

BIM4SMEs	A group for the smaller business
BIM4FM	A group for facilities managers
BIM2050	A group for the younger generation of construction industry professionals
BIM4 Private Sector Clients	A group for private sector clients
BIM For Retail	A groups for the retail industry
BIM4SupplySideDelivery	A group for product manufacturers, designers, contractors, specialist sub-contractors and other key members of the built environment
BIM4 Infrastructure (UK)	A group for road, bridges, water supply, sewers, electrical grids, telecommunications etc.
BIM4Water	A group for organisations in the water sector

Academia also has a strong presence. More than twenty academic institutions got involved with the BIM Hubs; many provided resource in the form of venues for Hub events and many are beginning to formulate new courses specialising in BIM. In the immediate future the BIM Task Group will be engaging with local authorities, which will introduce a new sector of interest. The form this will take is not defined at the time of writing

The specialist groups represent a focus on specific areas of the construction industry and the interest groups within it. There are a couple of groups which are worthy of special mention.

First the BIM2050 group is for the younger generation in the construction industry. The members of this group already have a different outlook on the way they see the industry working in the future. They are enthusiasts for more integration of the professions, the way they are educated and the way they operate in practice. More than that, they would readily adapt to a more co-operative rather than adversarial landscape in which to work. Their outlook is refreshing in comparison to many current embedded attitudes and hopefully they represent a beacon for future generations to follow.

The other group which is at the centre of the Government's initiative is BIM4FM. This group's intention is to engage everyone who is involved post Final Certificate. This would include, for example; facilities managers, maintenance people, those who carry out post-occupancy evaluations, those who recycle building stock, emergency services representatives. The list is endless. This is highly significant in that, after all, these are the people who will be involved in the use and upkeep of the facility which has been created.

They may well be the chief recipients of COBie information as mentioned elsewhere in the book.

Government Soft Landings BIM requirements

The Government Soft Landings (GSL) initiative attempts to create better outcomes for the building and infrastructure stock which the Government procures on our behalf. The Government spends billions on the buildings it procures for the benefit of the public and the Construction Strategy of May 2011 identified the need to improve the value offered by public sector construction. Soft Landings was identified as a way to improve performance of buildings and to meet the requirements of those who use them. It requires high quality and targeted information ('outputs') to inform future building strategies with an eye on outcomes. 'Outcomes' are the physical environment created by UK Construction Plc and 'outputs' are the media which it uses to communicate the what, how, why and when of what is created.

There are two key factors in effective GSL:

- Past experience gained from operation, maintenance and use informs early design stages of new projects.
- The design and construct stages provide the highest quality information for operation post Final Certificate.

GSL addresses the operational costs that Government faces, which usually far outweigh the capital cost of design and construction. The aspiration is to be better informed about the created facility and therefore better able to manage the magnitude of public expenditure on use, maintenance and recycling.

The GSL initiative goes along with the many explanations, definitions and approaches to BIM in that in one sense it does not care how the information it requires is provided as long as (and it is a big proviso) that information is of the highest possible quality and is focused on operation and all it includes.

The criteria for assessing information quality might include, for example, totally co-ordinated information on all external and internal works, reliable as-built information, complete maintenance and health and safety documentation and all manufacturers' product specifications. A formidable requirement.

As well as the rigour this implies the form of the information used in design and construction needs to be re-jigged to be useful to those who maintain, operate and use any given facility. This is not a trivial exercise.

The GSL hope is that BIM delivers a fully populated data set into computer-aided facility management systems (CAFM) thus reducing the resource required to do so. This supposes that there is a CAFM system out there that is capable of being 'fully populated', and that if there is it is capable of spanning the spectrum of use required by maintenance, operations and post-occupancy studies. There does seem to be an odd set of juxtapositions in the overall Government and GSL stream of thinking.

The introduction to BIM by Task Group personnel sends the message that BIM is not just 3D. This is an attempt to get away from the early historical explanations/definitions of BIM which had a heavy technological and 3D bias. By implication then BIM could include 2D and non-graphic information as well as 3D, as indeed it should. Throughout design and construction this mixture of 'Ds' does of course exist. We are then faced with the recommended method of transferring this information to maintainers, operators and users via the COBie format, which is essentially a spreadsheet; the 'Ds' structure is lost. The post-Final Certificate people need that information back in the appropriate 'D' or non-graphic form for them. It is not clear how all that multi-dimensional information will be resurrected in suitable 'Ds' for subsequent use by those who need it.

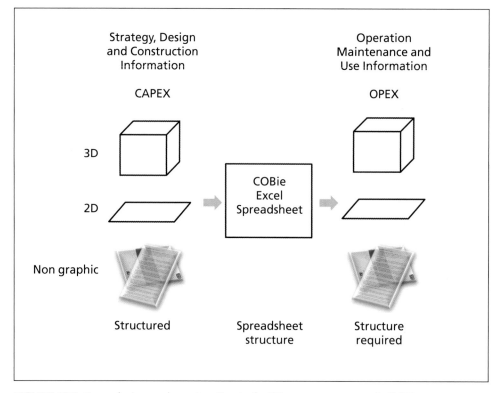

FIGURE 13.2 From design and construction to facilities management via COBie.

Non-graphic information may stand the best chance of making its way through the COBie spreadsheet to the 'other side'.

It appears to be a shame that pre-completion, project teams are being asked to be scrupulously careful about the structure and quality of their 3D and 2D information, which is then lost.

There have been several CAFM systems on the market since the 90s which could cope with 3D and 2D information. Some post-completion functions would benefit from that structure. For example, maintenance is often carried out in the less accessible spaces in a facility. An as-built 3D model would be useful in terms of evaluating access, maintenance clearance dimensions and health and safety requirements. Fire protection system schematics, signage, electrical layouts and landscape maintenance are very often depicted quite adequately in 2D.

It might have been more advantageous if the Government had put resource into preserving that information quality and structure created pre completion into post-completion stages. Perhaps support might be needed for those unfamiliar with the use, management and interpretation of 2D and 3D models. In all probability this approach would be no more onerous than that currently being suggested.

▶ **SUMMARY**

Government BIM

♦ The Government BIM initiative via its Task Group, Regional Hubs and special interest groups together with the publication of strategic documentation has provoked an unprecedented movement for cultural change in the construction industry.

♦ The formation of specialist groups, for example BIM4SMEs or the BIM2050 group for the younger generation of professionals, has ensured that every corner of the construction industry can be involved.

♦ PAS 1192, COBie, the CIC BIM Protocol and the RIBA Plan of Work 2013 provide a new rudimentary framework around which BIM communities can coalesce and develop.

♦ The RIBA Plan of Work 2013 and the BIM Overlay to the RIBA Outline Plan of Work give mainstream practice a framework for rigorous participation in the BIM-orientated Government procurement of projects.

♦ There is a UK-wide platform for participation in the development of the next level of BIM post 2016 via the BIM Hubs.

♦ On behalf of the public, BIM in conjunction with the Soft Landings programme will improve Government's capital and operational expenditure on its building stock and infrastructure assets.

SECTION 14
BIM in education

The importance of education

Education is certainly an extremely important issue and it is one of the most relevant sections in the Government's BIM report. It is crucial that:

- Mainstream practice educates itself so as not to be misled by some of the issues that are illustrated below.
- The purchaser needs to be educated in how to obtain proper BIM advantage through appropriate procurement documentation and legal expression.
- Higher education can play its part by integrating BIM principles into the curriculum for professional education and training.

Perhaps the most important groups of people to educate in the future as a matter of priority are the Government construction representatives and their procurement bodies. Historically CAD was 'left to its own devices' to find a level of understanding and application, and to a certain extent with confused and underused effect. Releasing national resources through a Government procurement initiative must ensure that the procurers have the very best understanding of the range of ingredients that BIM comprises and how they could be applied in a variety of ways within functional sectors in the public interest.

Paragraph 2.32 of the *Government Construction Policy*, published by the Cabinet Office in 2011, states 'Government will require fully collaborative 3D BIM (with all project and asset information, documentation and data being electronic) as a minimum by 2016'. Immediately, this gives a view of BIM skewed towards 3D modelling and the propaganda that all information can be stored on one software platform. Such statements will lead to difficulties when many benefits could be gained by taking a wider view of the full set of ingredients available under the BIM banner. Education is needed here to steer these reports towards embracing a full range of BIM possibilities and guide Government procurement bodies in all feasible directions.

Indeed to quote the Cabinet Office report again, 'Given the scale of the public sector construction programme, it is important to ensure that the Government commissioning teams are consistently equipped with the necessary high level of skills appropriate to specific projects and programmes.'

This is a very ambitious statement and requires a great deal of immediate investment in its own right. There are many individuals involved in health, education, transport, military and public leisure facilities procurement, for example, who need a significant amount of support in compiling suitable procurement documentation, which includes BIM techniques appropriate to their facilities, budgets and information asset requirements. Will it happen? Information technology and the part it plays in co-operative working are fully understood by only a small number of people. Formal professional education does not keep up with leading edge changes in technology or the development of skills required for integrated working.

Existing mid-career and senior staff need crash courses in co-operative working and information management if any immediate change is to be created. BIM should be an integral part of the higher and further education curricula for all the professions and trade groups. In terms of architects BIM does not feature significantly, if at all, in their education. The emphasis is predominantly on design given the RIBA's prescription that at least 50 per cent of an architectural student's activity should concentrate on 'design'. This deficiency needs to be addressed in the immediate future otherwise the architect will be deprived of yet another skill which should be an integral part of their knowledge and understanding. Currently professions are trained and educated within their own professional boundaries.

BIM and co-operative working require new skill sets which can only be achieved if there is some cross institutional co-operation on formulating curricula that transcend the boundaries.

Continuing Professional Development is a key component in providing existing practitioners, especially at senior levels, with insights into BIM. If they are to absorb these techniques into their business and project strategies then they need substantial support as soon as possible.

The current state of BIM in higher education

Current curricula fail us in that generally speaking there is little BIM content. In part this stems from the fact that there is a scarcity of suitable academics to teach the subject. This is partially due to the misconception among a proportion of academics that BIM is a highly technological subject. Therefore BIM does not figure significantly in most established education programmes.

The BIM movement which has developed over the past eighteen months or so at the time of writing has begun to generate a new demand for BIM education and glimpses of a refreshed provision begin to appear in certain younger academic establishments.

In practice BIM expectations differ quite widely. Some managers in practice are expecting newly qualified professionals to have been educated in the ways of BIM and are surprised to find they have no BIM expertise, not even covering the most basic and popular level of BIM technologies let alone all the other BIM ingredients. Another phenomenon is that the newly qualified, looking for first jobs, are asking practices if they are 'doing BIM'; if not, then they look for a job opportunity where BIM 'is being done' in the hope they will be educated in BIM or that they can implement what little BIM experience they have gained by themselves.

The traditional institutions are adapting much more slowly to new demands. Curriculum review and change tends to occur in protracted cycles and any changes take time to embed.

The need for education and training support in BIM is being identified by practice, industry and the younger generation rather than the traditional educational organisations. Enlightened members of the industry are already asking for graduates and other forms of qualified people to have some sort of BIM accreditation as part of their educational award.

The BIM Regional Hub launches throughout the UK have been interesting in that they have attracted the attendance of some of the younger educational establishments, which are keen to provide new courses centred on BIM.

There is an interesting observation to be made here in that these younger institutions are the direct academic equivalent of SMEs. The conventional wisdom/fear is that SMEs could be eclipsed by the large organisations in this new BIM world. The opposite of course is the case. SMEs are far more nimble on their feet than the 'big boys' and they can adjust to and adopt new methods much faster.

The same can be said of younger academic centres, where course design and validation can be carried out faster than the conventional cycles. They will attract the aspiring BIM professionals of the future and eclipse those academicians who do not adapt and evolve.

Integration is the keynote in education

Perhaps more importantly pedagogic structures in most cases do not provide for the collaboration and integration of approach that BIM requires. Educational institutions and the courses within them are as guilty of silo-ism as are the software vendors who provide the industry platforms that are deliberately limited in their ability to interact with each other. This has happened because historically trades and professions have created educational courses around their own subject area, for example design, quantity take off, structural design and environmental design, leaving it to the time they enter practice to put all these areas of expertise together. Of course the final outcome in the form of a built facility has to be a successful amalgam of everyone's effort. Education needs to acknowledge the integration that this requires.

It's a matter for conjecture and hope as to where the solutions to both software and educational problems will come from. These trends are inhibiting the development of a richer BIM environment for the construction industry.

Integration must be a major future determinant in future pedagogic models and content irrespective of whether it is related to BIM education. The need is obvious if UK Construction Plc and its attendant professions and trades are to be competitive internationally.

In the context of the Government's BIM initiative more integration in education could and should have a significant role in shaping what 'Level 3' should look like. If the UK is to maximise its growth opportunities in a global arena then its educational system must supply the next generation of leaders.

▶ SUMMARY

BIM in education

- A new interdisciplinary integrated pedagogic model is required to educate the next generation of professionals.

- Current pedagogic models are guilty of silo-ism, just like the software vendors.

- The class of several million in the construction industry represents a very big educational challenge which requires a diverse response.

- There is a demand for better BIM education both from practices and from students wanting better job prospects.

- Educational establishments at all levels must equip themselves with the staff who understand BIM concepts and who can therefore provide a robust BIM education.

- BIM must be acknowledged as a course of study in its own right and not just a 'bolt-on' to something else.

- There needs to be some innovation in providing BIM course content that services educational needs both now and in the future.

SECTION 15
Where will BIM go in the future?

The political landscape

Mainstream practice in the UK is beginning to enjoy a level of evangelism and enthusiasm for BIM that has been extant in the USA for some time. America benefits from a larger scale of market, larger projects and vast public procurement agencies that the UK does not. As early as July 2009 the State of Wisconsin declared all new building with a capital value in excess of $5m should 'begin their A/E design processes with BIM and 3D software'. The stimulus for this came from an earlier Executive Order which required state agencies to conform to higher environmental and energy efficiency standards. The UK is now catching up, not only in terms of championing BIM, but also using environmental issues as a lever.

There are now three significant reports, namely:

- *BIM: Management for Value, Cost and Carbon Improvement. A report for the Government Construction Client Group:* BIM Working Party.
- Cabinet Office: *Government Construction Strategy*.
- *Low Carbon Construction:* Innovation and Growth Team, HM Government.

These reports are valuable in that their main benefit is to raise the profile of BIM in the UK and to consolidate much BIM thinking from the past couple of decades.

The reports have been substantially underpinned by the publication of the following protocols which support the adoption and promotion of BIM processes.

- PAS 1192
- COBie
- CIC BIM Protocol
- RIBA Plan of Work 2013

The Government as body politic and procurement agent can potentially revolutionise the face of the UK construction industry. It is not the intention here to review these publications in depth, but several key issues have to be faced in the future.

Eliminate the rhetoric

The conventional and historic rhetoric from those in government circles should be superseded by a decisive, simple and well-thought-out strategy for change in the way information is managed in construction. Fragmented structure, statistics, supply chain issues, characteristics of architecture and the construction industry, barriers, enablers and drivers have all been well documented in the past; it is time to move on and actually achieve something.

There are committees in abundance and we all know how the camel came about. It is difficult to avoid in the reports the traditional dichotomy of cost against value. The rhetoric possesses an uneasy tension. Should BIM be an instrument for driving costs down in the future, or if a wider connotation on BIM is acknowledged, then BIM might be a vehicle for achieving value in whole life cycle costing.

Environmental issues also play a part in the rhetoric. Of course carbon efficiency can be integrated into design irrespective of whether BIM techniques are used or not. Many organisations who have never heard of BIM are doing so at the present time. Alternatively other serious topics such as overseas development and emergency practice or the regeneration of brownfield sites might be used as drivers for BIM. BIM is a valid topic in its own right and should be considered as such in the future. Many laudable areas of endeavour could be assisted by its application.

The reports tend to express the right things, but day-to-day life does not seem to follow through on the practicalities and pragmatics of moving to a new state. Do the reports actually reflect the position, understanding and outlook of the small to medium sized mainstream practice or are they conversations among the 'big boys'?

Outcomes

The focus tends to be on outcomes. There is a vast amount of resource required, techniques invented and attitudes changed to achieve some of the objectives which the reports refer to or are implied by their content. Serious investment is required in techniques that are essential in supporting future aspirations for BIM working. For example, the interoperability concept underlies and is crucial to much of what is discussed in terms of easier and more efficient information flows. The software vendors have kept their own silo approach to this issue. Other organisations who are trying to achieve common languages and standards on this front are vastly underfunded in relation to the value of the national and global construction market and the importance that Government professes to place on future BIM working. Government could in effect 'nationalise' work on interoperability by channelling funds through the British Standards Institution, the BRE, or professional institutions, for example, to build interoperability in the interests of all stakeholders. This would relieve the industry from the financial burden of having to self fund what is otherwise a significant overhead.

Alternatively, research channels through the Technology Strategy Board and the EPSRC could receive an enormous boost. Orders of magnitude of increase are required if the 2016 targets are to be met with the levels of information management that the reports hope will be possible. Architecture and construction receive relatively small amounts of research funding in comparison to the aerospace industry, for example.

Unfortunately many aspects of electronic information management are not fully understood by those requiring it to be used, nor is it an attractive subject area whose importance is immediately obvious. The part that electronic information management plays in BIM should be given higher priority and more resource if many of the ideas in reports are to be achieved.

Business proposition

If there were to be a comparison made with commercial strategy then any business planning a major investment would think roughly in terms of making a loss in the first year, breaking even in the second and gaining profit or benefit in the third. This analogy could translate into the Government's thinking on BIM initiatives. The Government could provide financial incentives, freedom from litigation, project insurance or accreditations to companies willing to expend valuable resource to the cause of a better profession and industry. Companies could be assisted in exploring business change in terms of different fee profiles across work stages, the establishment of new value-added services and the redistribution of resources that a BIM environment will require.

The Government would break even when a critical mass of effort had shown a degree of success in terms of producing benefit from the use of BIM methodologies. Individual participants would have to come forward with the benefits as perceived by them. Yardsticks for proving benefit are difficult if not impossible to establish because each project tends to be a prototype, even on building typologies such as hospitals or schools. Site conditions, local policies, different budget pockets are just a few examples of influences that tend to militate against benchmarking and consistent metrics.

It is not simply a case of driving costs down. The break-even point would establish where costs could be legitimately reduced but where expenditure should be increased in the interests of overall life cycle benefit. These new approaches require a complete overhaul in financial thinking during project life cycle rather than a belief that costs can be driven ever further down. The final 'profit' or benefit comes when confidence and knowledge in implementing BIM have been acquired by the majority of the industry.

This would represent a true investment in the future. It is a step in the right direction for Government to make declarations and change its procurement policies and processes but Government initiatives have a tendency to expect the industry itself to shoulder the costs and Government to reap the benefits.

Other agencies

Government might influence other agencies within its jurisdiction that could have an enormous catalytic effect on the uptake and sophisticated use of BIM. Building Regulations, CDM legislation, public building sector guides and planning policies and authorities are all rich seams of information to be referred to and utilised on all projects no matter what scale. These agencies might begin to assemble their information in a way that conforms to some kind of standard so that relevant regulation, recommendations and policies are readily absorbed into the BIM environment.

Much of their information could be incorporated into clever objects that performed various checking and commentary functions when delivered into the BIM pool of activity and knowledge. That information could be incorporated into designs and, if structured according to BIM principles, could form the basis of the information submitted for approvals. Indeed, if created properly these objects could carry out a certain amount of checking within the BIM environment prior to applications being made, thus reducing the resource required by the regulatory or planning agency.

The cultural landscape

Behavioural change in the future is as important as political or technological change, perhaps even more so. Architects, other professions, contractors and suppliers have deeply embedded working practices and long standing delineations of professional responsibility and liability. Currently each participant believes they have optimised their work processes, the way they accumulate information within their domain and their use of existing technology.

Countless project delivery methods and contractual relationships have created an atmosphere in which it is difficult for the seeds of BIM to be sown and flourish. Demanding project schedules, client budgets and an iterative design process militate against finding resource to address different work practices and technological techniques. This more than anything has to change. Information management across the entire project life cycle requires new skill sets and attitudes. To achieve a single quality controlled information repository for any scale of project requires an outlook on project team working that is only possessed by a minority at the moment.

If BIM is to be successful in fulfilling the Government aspirations then project teams will need people who can display a willingness to adapt and acquire new skill sets, possibly several times within their careers. Earlier in this book some indications were given on how to identify people and companies who display team working potential. Project team strategists, designers, constructors, operators and users must interchange understanding of their respective work processes, skill sets and knowledge bases if the information they produce is to be properly quality controlled, integrated and trusted as a long term asset.

The future must see a creation of a team approach, support for new ideas, a no-blame atmosphere, distributed decision making, changing leadership focus over time and newer forms of contract and insurance. Teams will become more distributed as the web and other technologies make it easier, and more desirable for the planet, to move around information rather than people. This places a call on information to be quality controlled under common conventions upon its creation, and interoperability to be improved by orders of magnitude if it is to be moved around reliably. Technology should become more inconspicuous, less compartmentalised and should be a servant to the project rather than a neurosis for keeping up with the latest bell and whistle or, worse still, a pressure to divert investment unnecessarily towards the system the procurer demands.

Autonomous but co-operative pools of skill sets, knowledge and technological support should operate in the best interests of the project rather than those of individual people and companies. Skill pools would group and regroup as required through each stage of a project and from project to project. Physical presence might be anywhere on the planet. A change of emphasis could be facilitated from business to project. Small or large practices may be formed in the same town or across continents by like-minded co-operative individuals who believe in teamwork and can manage information at an unprecedented level.

The technological future

Technology does of course facilitate the way architectural practice and other members of the construction industry implement their own particular state of mind now and in the future. Available technology will influence how their BIM mind will develop.

The immediate future

The immediate future is relatively easy to predict. The scope of software products will broaden, more functionality related to individual disciplines and specialisms will be provided. The sophistication of objects and parametrics will increase, but whether it can be harnessed to its full potential remains to be seen. More and more applications will come to market supporting the supply chains in terms of lean inventory, off-site manufacture, fit first time and sub-assembly production.

Sustainability and carbon foot-printing will form a greater part of the BIM environment. Clients who are more environmentally conscious will expect better predictability of energy performance and revenue costs, which in turn will rely on finding building products that have a better environmental performance.

Clever product information

Product manufacturers have concentrated their efforts promoting their products on the web in terms of high quality graphics, downloadable technical information and video presentations of their products in production and use. Perhaps they will gradually turn their attentions from supplying standard details in DWG, DXF or .pdf formats to more sophisticated forms of delivery.

The possibility of delivering components as objects direct to CAD/BIM platforms has been there for some years. Doing this would consume relatively little resource in percentage terms within the PR and marketing budgets spent by product manufacturers. For some reason providing their product in this way is not being exploited as quickly as technology could permit. There are some significant issues that may provide reasons for preventing intelligent product information delivery. First there is a question of professional responsibility. If the product can evaluate the context it finds itself in, and furthermore it can adjust itself to the designer's constraints perhaps beyond the manufacturer's specification, then who takes responsibility and how is the responsibility audit trail established?

Versioning is another problem. Product manufacturers are constantly improving their offering. A designer might include a particular version of a product, but as we know the project may be delayed for some time, months perhaps even years. The version embedded in the design history in terms of costings, reports to the client and drawing revisions, for example, may no longer be available. How long does the product manufacturer keep a version, or is there delay and cost due to a major component revision?

BIMs and BEMs

We have explored how BIM can be seen as a specific software platform or as a wider interpretation of holistic information management through project life cycle. Within that span of outlook a subsidiary notion of a Building Element Model (BEM) is developing. BEM is as elusive as BIM in the way the terminology is being applied. At one end of a spectrum BEM is being used to mean an individual building product incorporating its entire manufacturer's specification information. Geometry may or may not be part of the package at this level. More useful applications of BEM do certainly include geometry as well as possible relationship descriptions.

Advanced applications of BEM represent a component product as sub-assemblies. For example, a BEM might contain information about a cladding panel component. It might also contain information about its bracketry and secondary steelwork connections to primary structure. 'Intelligence' about the way the panel can be spaced and optimally sized could also be part of the package.

Finally BEM has a connotation as part of a larger BIM – a smaller element of a larger whole. The idea has validity in the sense that the practical world, as we have seen previously, consists of several 'pools' of information linked together by the best means available from the software platforms used. All this will add to the information soup that is BIM. BEM may be a transitory expression used temporarily until BIM is better understood and implemented.

Unless there is better co-operation between software developers on the compatibility and exchange of 'behaviour' then information and 'activity' contained within the BIM will be limited by compartmentalisation and will to some extent defeat the object of BIM.

Waiting for inventions

However much we might wonder at the constant march of IT and marvel at the phenomenon of the web, the 'soft' or software technology that we use, as opposed to 'hard' technology, such as communications, mobile phones and of course small and more powerful computers, is based on a handful of concepts; objects, URLs, an http page and some protocols. It is disarmingly simple.

Every industry sector and academic interest group has invented what it believes to be a form of those basic concepts which best suits its needs. There are myriad manifestations; many computer programming languages breathe life into them, tens of thousands of applications and subsidiary and supporting concepts and protocols have now made for a complex world predicated on simplicity.

What might loosely be called the software industry, meaning pure software engineering itself as well as all the other public and private, large and small organisations that create software, have utilised and developed these basic concepts within their own industry domain. Social sciences, biological sciences, commerce, medicine and manufacturing industries of all types, to name but a few, have made use of these basic concepts.

Journeys into fuzzy logics, explorations in mathematics, such as prime number searches or set theories, for example, will continue to help the BIM environment. How? In the former case by providing us with more ability to build and interpret relationships between things such as building components, contract clauses and energy evaluation and code compliance. Prime number searches help to match patterns in text and provide encryption and de-encryption techniques, which are necessary for providing unique audit trails on graphic and non-graphic information as well as secure transmissions of information.

There are two emerging phenomena that will have a likely effect on the way everyone uses their computer in conjunction with the web in the longer term future. BIM, in any shape or form, will be no exception. For some, these trends will be treacherous, mysterious and contrary to the way they perceive architectural endeavour. To others they will offer a fascinating new series of opportunities in a world where virtuality as a methodology and as a team member becomes integrated into the cultures of architecture and construction.

Cloud computing has been mentioned earlier and it is likely that the trend to use computing power 'out there somewhere' will continue at an increasingly rapid rate. An emerging phenomenon is something called the semantic web – Tim Berners-Lee is attributed with inventing the idea.

Currently we enter a word or phrase into a search engine. We get many results. We look at a particular result page, our eyes dart around searching for the information we want rather that the old fashioned method of reading from left to right, top to bottom. Embedded within the page we find links to other web pages that the search engine believes might help us. We interpret the meaning of the information presented to us and decide where to go next. The key point is that at the moment a great deal of human browsing and interpretation is required to extract relevant information, integrate information from various sources and combine it with the software platforms and information repositories that are used on a day-to-day basis.

In future the semantic web offers the ability to understand language better and moreover the context in which it is being used. Information we find on the web page will be able to make decisions and enquire further on our behalf, hence the virtual team member. The cloud then becomes a place where problems can be solved and more and more services accessed. The semantic web and the cloud will transform the web into a brain rather than a search with human interpretation. It is all about making information work for us instead of simply finding information.

Google – the sleeping giant for architecture and construction?

If Google's intention to become the gatekeeper of all information becomes a reality, then entries into specific industry sectors might be on the horizon. Certainly architecture and construction are rich seams of ever increasing global information and therefore must be a subject of interest for the kings of information. Building Regulations, CDM Regulations, planning policies, product specifications, codes of practice and guidance notes are just a few of the information domains that might come under the Google spotlight.

Google 3D Warehouse is a new web site where anyone can upload, download and share 3D models of anything. There is no restriction on use of the models; they can be downloaded and modified by providing additional information or made to do something by the attaching software applications. Combining some of these strands together in new ways presents some intriguing prospects. If, for example, Google picked up the baton for architecture and construction and threw hundreds of its software engineers at the information and interoperability questions, as it could well do, we would be subjected to a revolution that many attitudes would be challenged to accommodate.

Google's relative speed of operation and reliable implementation of web technology would brush aside most of what has gone already, in terms of technology, information standards and information flows. The expectation that everyone on the project team would use the same technology platform would be solved not by pressure to purchase the same system but simply by using the ubiquitous Google Built Environment alongside Google Apps, Google Earth, Google Docs and Google Maps. Versioning and interoperability would become a thing of the past. Currently Google updates the software driving its search engine many times a month without the world noticing; all players would be on the same level pitch. This tends to put our current practice of purchasing updates and struggling with data transfers across software platforms in the shade.

Take this with developments in the semantic web and we move from information to intelligent information. Far more interaction between product manufacturers, regulatory authorities, client groups, project teams and supply chains would be possible. Pools of virtual information would 'understand' each other. Autonomous but co-operative virtual agents carrying knowledge and actions would be injected into the BIM environment.

The future of BIM does not lie with further revisions of current software platforms but with a combination of a Google-like environment outlined above, a legal atmosphere which is even more co-operative than the current positive forms of contract and education leading to a proper understanding of the genuine and diverse ingredients and techniques that might be used in a BIM context.

BIM in the future: security and virtuality

The future for BIM in construction is an intriguing area for conjecture. Paul Morrell's original declaration and the current flurry of activity prompted by the use of the acronym BIM has served a very useful purpose. The Government's BIM initiative has provoked a long overdue reaction in terms of stimulating the construction industry to reappraise the way it works collectively on projects.

As BIM develops and becomes more collaborative it will by its very nature be more available 'in the cloud' and thus there will need to be a clearer understanding of cyber threats and security solutions.

The Common Data Environment alluded to in Government BIM documentation and the wider adoption of the internet as a means of implementing a BIM project team environment are areas where new cyber vigilance needs to be understood and applied. Traditional software platforms used in the construction industry are already beginning to offer cloud solutions, which on the one hand puts project information in a more collaborative form than ever before, but on the other subjects it to a vulnerability that previous generations of project teams have never known.

Virtuality will hit the BIM environment via routes other than the traditional 'CAD' software platforms used by the construction industry.

Offshoots from the BIM data set, for example planning and building regulation applications, BREEAM evaluations, health and safety and operations manuals, will all become virtual information and as such more exposed and accessible to the effects of virtuality.

2D, 3D or non-graphic product manufacturer information used in the BIM model will exist in the cloud and the virtual product based on object technology discussed earlier in the book will be just as accessible to cyber attack.

The development of virtuality raises many questions in the BIM environment, for example what effect will there be on professional and contractual responsibilities or the protection of project information. At the moment there are no ready answers but what we must do is to get these issues on the agenda so that solutions can be found.

In a historical context the BIM acronym has played its part as a catalyst for change although of itself it is no more than a passing device. Virtuality will be a far more potent agent for change in the future.

The following sections highlight the emerging phenomena in a virtual world which will have an impact on our project BIM communities.

Francis Maude's cyber security statements and policy

The internet has grown spectacularly since its arrival for public consumption in 1991. It can be a force for good in the way it connects people across the globe in an entirely new and powerful way, but it can also be quite sinister. Cyber crime is still in at an embryonic stage in its development but is already having an effect on UK business and is probably set to have an even greater impact as cyber criminals exploit the current difficulties in tracking them down.

Two milestone reports, one from Cambridge University in 2012 (*Measuring the Cost of Cybercrime:* Ross Anderson, Chris Barton, Rainer Böhme, Richard Clayton, Michel J. G. van Eeten, Michael Levi, Tyler Moore, Stefan Savage) and one commissioned by the Cabinet Office from Detica in 2011 (*The Cost of Cybercrime:* A Detica report in partnership with the Office of Cyber Security and Information Assurance in the Cabinet Office), a company owned by BAE Systems which specialises in information security, put the cost of cyber crime in the UK at £18bn and £27bn respectively. Their figures are the subject of some discussion, but whether out by large factors the cost to industry is very high indeed by any standard. The reports' findings prompted Francis Maude, the Minister responsible for cyber action, to launch a £650m initiative up to 2015 to help combat cyber crime within the UK. This was followed in 2013 by his Cyber Security Information Partnership, a partnership between industry and Government to combat cyber threats.

The Government BIM initiative aims towards a target of BIM Level 3 from 2016 onwards. At the moment the nature of Level 3 is something that is being discussed by the various Task Group groups together with feedback from BIM Regional Hubs. What is certain is that the nature of Level 3 will inevitably involve a degree of virtuality. General practice which is involved with Government procurement cycles will have to keep up with this. Practice otherwise will be under pressure to improve/change BIM methods to keep pace.

The implications of Level 3 in this context are twofold and in some senses opposed. First the ability to co-operate and be more open will be enhanced with virtual BIM environments that have better information transportation, integration and sharing capabilities. However that improved position must be protected by finding the most secure cloud hosts with strict access control.

Perhaps the adaptation of social media concepts and access to BIM information models via mobile devices will offer even more options for co-operation but this will also increase the need for more security.

The hacking threat and BIM

Hacking will grow into big business unless the internet is policed in some way. Firewalls and so-called anti-virus software are simple training exercises for most serious hackers. The only form of security is simply the hope that nobody bothers with you. A recent survey showed that even what is thought of as the best anti-virus software in the world has only a 10–25 per cent success rate in interception, let alone removal. If hackers are determined and can see a business opportunity then very few systems, even military ones are safe at the moment.

There is little global agreement as to how the internet should be governed. Is it governable?

So what is the prospect for architecture and construction? A mundane starting point is the ARB's Architects Code, where standard 4.3 states:

You should ensure that adequate security is in place to safeguard both paper and electronic records for your clients, taking full account of data protection legislation, and that clients' confidential information is safeguarded.

The clients' electronic records are vulnerable to attack. How can any architect be expected to provide safeguards? At one end of the spectrum a court might implement the usual test of 'reasonableness', in other words what would any architect do in the same circumstances. The answer would be that they had put in place the necessary backup procedures, firewall and anti-virus protection; technically a good defence given the courts' current understanding of matters virtual. Action under the Code might be dismissed on this basis, that the test of 'reasonableness' was satisfied.

However, despite these procedures, a client may still have suffered considerable loss due to hacking. Could they sue the architect on these grounds? In the BIM environment the architect has a specific responsibility placed upon them by this standard in their Code of Conduct. Should or could the client or the architect obtain insurance to cover against these sorts of cyber attack?

PAS 1192, the BIM Protocol and the BIM movement in general have generated the notion of the BIM Information Manager. PAS 1192 defines the role of Information Management in a BIM context as 'Tasks and procedures applied to inputting, processing and generation activities to ensure accuracy and integrity of information'. At the moment the definition does not explicitly concern itself with cyber security, however a wide interpretation of 'integrity' could include that aspect. The formulation of BIM Level 3 may have a more conspicuous approach to the problem.

The Information Manager task may fall to one of the traditional roles such as lead designer, the contractor or the client themself. Whose responsibility it is depends on how appointments and contracts are framed. Whoever it is must be aware of the hacking threat so that the best available protection is obtained.

There are many sinister implications of hacking. For example if a BIM team is working on a sensitive project such as a Ministry of Defence installation or an airport, information passed around as e-mails or in the BIM environment based on web-based collaborative portals could be intercepted, the information copied and sold to terrorist organisations.

Anyone working on Ministry of Justice projects could have their information intercepted and sold to the criminal fraternity. Anyone working on hospitals or Clinical Commissioning Group projects could have their information intercepted and sold to the drugs cartels.

The above are perhaps extreme examples of what hackers might get up to. At a more everyday level, misplaced hacking activity might be simply the alteration of tender figures in an electronic communication; changes to information revisions to avoid or provoke litigation might happen on collaborative portals; one product specification might be replaced by another.

In a future virtualised world, architects in particular will need to be aware of the obligation placed upon them by standard 4.3 of the Architect's Code but all members of the BIM project team will need to take hacking on board as a threat to their collective effort. In the Government context, given some of the sensitive building stock it presides over it is essential that a secure and reliable information asset is delivered by the BIM team. In future the construction industry in general and all BIM environments in particular need to take hacking as seriously as it is taken in the online banking world.

Big Data and virtual agents

Elsewhere this book gives a brief insight into objects and the semantic web. If we put these two concepts together we have the ability to carry and analyse information, understand its meaning and do something with it. This is a part of human behaviour.

When computers first appeared frequently heard comments would be 'computers cannot think', 'computers will never make decisions'. Even in today's world these comments have been superseded. Google analyses tweet messages for phraseology, emphases, connotations, inferences, expressions of emotion, fear, kindness etc. The World Wide Web Consortium oversees and develops standards for the semantic content of the web. These two powerful organisations have succeeded in drastically changing our social and business lives with the ideas they have invented and implemented.

Big Data is a phenomenon that we must add into the mixture of developments which will shape the future of virtuality, and virtuality for the construction industry in particular. Statistics for the amount of information we create on the web are staggering.

Gigabytes	1,000,000,000	
Terabytes	1,000,000,000,000	1,000 Gigas
Petabytes	1,000,000,000,000,000	1,000 Teras
Exabytes	1,000,000,000,000,000,000	1,000 Petas
Zettabytes	1,000,000,000,000,000,000,000	1,000 Exas
Yottabytes	1,000,000,000,000,000,000,000,000	1,000 Zettas

FIGURE 15.1 The inexorable growth of the volume of data.

The above figure shows the levels of information that agencies somewhere out there on the web are working with now. Where once we talked about gigabytes, terms such as 'yottabytes' have had to evolve to define unchartered territory in levels of data generation. Social media, government agencies, transportation systems, space and medical research to name but a few represent areas of human endeavour which are amassing data at a frightening rate and in incomprehensible volumes.

In 2012 IBM claimed that we create 2.5 quintillion bytes (1 exabyte equals 1 quintillion bytes) of data every day and that 90 per cent of the data in the world today has been created in the last two years.

There are several important ideas to be grasped from the Big Data movement. First, there is no limit to the volume of data that can now be analysed. In the past the only possibility was to sample data and declare assumptions and warn about sample inaccuracies. Now there is no need for this. The entire information set that is in focus can be analysed.

Speed too is important where critical decisions have to be taken quickly. Emerging Big Data access methods and increased computing power mean that data can be reached almost instantaneously.

Big Data enables varieties of information conventionally kept separate to be analysed as one coherent whole, for example sensor data, audio, video and click patterns as well as BIM information. As a consequence correlations otherwise thought impossible may be discovered and questions answered that were previously thought to be beyond reach.

An important characteristic of Big Data is that there is no need for rigid information structures. Information needs only to be labelled with as many labels as its author wishes. This relies on the author providing the necessary labels for all the purposes the information might service. The randomness that labelling might inflict on databases is the new problem of inaccuracy and replaces the old problem of sample inaccuracies.

Big Data has some downsides. For example, BIM models need to be integrated to an extent not yet achieved otherwise unreliable correlations might be made. Haphazard labelling of information may lead to spurious correlations which might misdirect decision making based on Big Data findings. The new world of Big Data needs to be approached with some care for the time being.

There is already evidence that virtual agents are on their way. The Coronet project for the Singapore Government, started way back in the mid 1990s, set out to show that automated building regulations checking was a possibility. Over the years this project has illustrated that the reality is getting closer and closer. Autodesk's Ecotect Analysis product could be reinvented as an independent virtual agent to inspect BIM models in terms of their energy consumption and thermal performance, for example.

Let us see how some of these concepts might percolate into architecture and construction.

Traditionally information about a project, from its inception through design, construction and into use and maintenance, has been held in databases in a relatively piecemeal way on a large number of disparate software systems with diverse functions throughout project life cycle. The future promises a gradual merging of this information into a bigger integrated whole.

We are an information society. Information about the behaviour of new products, post-occupancy evaluations, more stringent health and safety regulation, to take just three examples, illustrate the burgeoning information phenomenon in construction. Hopefully the more information there is available, the better informed is decision making in providing better outcomes for the built environment.

As a consequence the cloud-based BIM database will increase in volume and complexity at an exponential rate. Huge BIM files will become part of the Big Data scene and will provide new challenges of compilation, accessibility and quality control.

Vast tracts of the Building Regulations, planning policies, contract documents and health and safety documentation are simply information, relationships between pieces of information and guidance on doing something, all things which objects and the semantic web can easily cope with. Any web-based regulatory or legal documentation could be 'understood' by software platforms and used in a virtual BIM environment to test for compliance.

For example a virtual building inspector could visit your BIM environment and inspect your design, highlighting areas which do not comply with regulations. Not only that, the virtual agent can 'understand' your design. If it tests and finds it non-compliant it knows the correct rules and can modify your design to comply. Robots equipped with cameras and sensors could be stationed on site to monitor compliance. This raises lots of questions, for instance where does this leave you in terms of the latest version shown to your client, but more importantly how does it affect your professional responsibilities? It could potentially degrade professional standards as a level of building inspection expertise is no longer required.

A similar situation might be encountered with a virtual planning officer. The virtual agent could access your design on your software platform and vet your proposals to see if they conform to planning policies. For example the transport policies seen on many planning authority web sites give information for pedestrian access, public and emergency vehicle access and parking densities. Information, doing something, relationships between items of information, and semantics of a particular domain are all ripe for transformation into object technology and virtualisation. However, once again this could lead to a level of planning expertise disappearing.

A contract contains legal phraseologies, time limits and key words such as 'shall', 'may', 'divergences' and 'discrepancies'. The semantics surrounding these key expressions can be scrutinised, relationships established internally between clauses and possibly with information contained within external software platforms such as BIM platforms. The virtual contract could be equipped with the ability to (remember, objects can 'do things') monitor, issue directions, eliminate inconsistencies between different contracts on a project, or instigate legal action if it finds via connections to other platforms that a party is in breach. A startling proposition, but not beyond the realms of possibility. In this case we might be happy if a certain amount of legal expertise does disappear.

Similar ideas can be applied to health and safety regulations, briefing statements, BREEAM assessments, insurance policies and the CO_2 police for example. Virtual agents could also influence off-site manufacturing.

The product manufacturer sponsored by a bigger information collection agency might collect all the details about our searches for their products and similar ones. The custodian of that information and the agency that produces the virtual intelligent product becomes the power broker. Their virtual product might influence our design and modify the context in which the product operates. It could modify our design to provide the optimum conditions for itself. This may conflict with other products and their performance and the architects' and contractors' obligations of duty of care and fitness for purpose.

The information agent could collect all information about their product from all installations worldwide. Amassing information and modifying software platforms which design and install the product at a faster pace than is now possible would also become a powerful tool. It would be more useful than the product itself to the manufacturer in that the pressures which presently exist to keep up with the current version would mean the manufacturer could always exert pressure on getting the next newer model.

The same time information would be used to drive automatic manufacturing and installation processes and a level of employment would be eliminated.

A final thought in this section is the potential benefit of Big Data on future construction and urban planning. If we take post-occupancy evaluations, for example, there is no need to restrict ourselves to the sample feedback from one hospital on how it met its aspirations for patient satisfaction. All hospitals in the UK, Europe or the entire world can be taken into account if necessary. Google or some other agency not yet invented may be recommending how we build our hospitals.

In an urban context social interaction information could be collected on crime, property values, neighbourliness, popular schools, shopping facilities, transportation systems and what constitutes 'good environment'. This Big Data could be used by any positive or negative agency to shape the future of our towns and cities.

It is time to believe that far more abilities, techniques and functionalities are coming our way, more than was ever envisaged as being possible, twenty, ten or even five years ago given some of these radical new ideas. All of them have a severely profound effect on the way we as architects will work in future, far more profound than the current BIM fracas. That is if there is such a thing as an architect in the future.

► SUMMARY

Where will BIM go in the future?

- There has been enough discussion about BIM by Government and the industry generally, it is now time for action.

- Government could 'nationalise' interoperability with an orchestrated programme of funded development via BRE, BSI, the professional institutions and academia.

- Government should ensure its own procurers are educated in the ways of BIM.

- Government should view BIM in construction as a typical three phase business cycle, i.e. investment/pain, break-even and then benefit, instead of giving out a one-dimensional message saying that costs should be driven down.

- UK Construction Plc could use information management as a powerful catalyst in a significant cultural move towards more co-operative forms of working.

- In the immediate future product manufacturers could take advantage of existing technology to deliver the entire product model or BEM (building element model).

- Cloud computing and the semantic web will offer opportunities which are an anathema to some and exciting to others; either way, significant change is on its way in a virtual world.

- Google could invent a completely different paradigm for software development in the future.

- Cyber security should be on the agenda because BIM environments will reside more and more in the cloud, where cyber attacks will increase in frequency and have greater impact on project information.

- Virtuality will create new challenges for professional roles and responsibilities.

- UK Construction Plc should be the thought leader for cyber security.

- Virtual agents may be a new participant in the way our BIM environments are shaped and behave.

- The ability to appraise vast volumes of data in strategic design, construction and facility usage may lead to better outcomes for the built environment in the future.

Conclusion

This book is an attempt to waylay some of the fears about BIM that may be extant at the moment in mainstream practice. The expression 'mainstream practice' has been used often to symbolise the fact that all of BIM's tenets are as useful to the small practice as to the large organisations who tend to monopolise discussions. BIM is not just for the big players.

The BIM acronym with its annoyingly ambiguous, elusive but all encompassing and intriguing meaning is fuelling one of the most interesting phases in architecture and construction. It is ensuring that cherished assumptions are being challenged and new horizons sought. We have been brought to a point where we must believe there is a better way of intervening in the built environment than fragmented knowledge, wasted resource and law suits. BIM will touch everyone concerned with the built environment. Fantastic opportunities beckon.

Index

added value 63–5
American Institute of Architects 18, 109–11
Architects Code: Standards of Conduct and Practice 65–6

behavioural change 32–3, 140–1
benefits 30, 51, 68–9
Big Data 150–1
BIM Execution Plan (BEP) 121
BIM Industry Working Group 19
BIM Protocol 123–4
BIM Regional Hubs 21, 126–28, 135
BIM Task Group 21, 119, 120
BIM2050 group 128
BIM4FM 128
BS1192 (2007) 47, 63
Building Element Model (BEM) 142–3
Building Information Modeling Protocol Exhibit (BIM-PE) 18, 109–11
business case 51–7
business opportunities 63–6

CAD (computer-aided design) 35–7
champions 80–1
change management 61–2, 82, 105
CI/SfB Construction Indexing Manual 47–8, 63
classification systems 47–9
client perspectives 67–71
cloud computing 44, 144
COBie (Construction Operations Building Information Exchange) 122–3
Code of Professional Conduct 65–6
collaborative contracts 113–16
collaborative working 61, 70, 77–79, 114–15, 141
commercial benefits 63–6
computer-aided design (CAD) 35–7
computer-aided facility management systems (CAFM) 129, 130
Construction Industry Council (CIC) 123–4
contracts 32, 109, 113–16

co-ordinate systems 96–7
costs 52–3, 69, 139
cultural change 32–3, 117–18, 140–1
cyber security 147–49

data exchange 95–7
data security 66, 108, 147–49
definitions of BIM 16–18, 23–4
design briefs 64–5

economic recession 20
educational issues 69–70, 133–6 (*see also* training)
exchange formats 92–3, 93–4
expertise 60, 64, 65–6, 107–8
extranets 41

facilities management 129–30
fees 63–4, 65
financial benefits 63–6
forms of appointment 64–5
forms of contract 22, 32, 109, 113–14

General Services Administration (GSA) 17, 67
global market 21
Google 144–5
Government Construction Client Group 19
government policy 133–4, 137
government procurement 19, 21, 69–70, 119–31, 133–4
Government Soft Landings (GSL) 128–30

handover documentation 68–9
higher education 134–5
human resources 79–81 (*see also* project teams)
    management of 109
    remuneration 53–4
    roles and responsibilities 60, 87, 102, 106–9, 124, 148–9

implementation 77–112 (*see also* human
   resources)
     change management 61–2, 82, 105
     convergence plan 95–102
     information standards 46–9, 81, 90–5
     management process 85–7, 103–6
     pilot projects 67–8, 102
     practice size 57–9, 100, 106
     system development 104
information agents 151–3
information exchange 93–4, 120–3
information handover 68–9
information management 55–6, 104–5
information manager role 107, 124, 148–49
information precision 98
information preparation and review 100–1,
   104–5
information standards 46–9, 81, 90–5
information structuring 63, 90–1, 99
information types 29–30, 92–3
Infrastructure as a Service (IaaS) 44–5
integrated BIM (iBIM) 25
Integrated Project Team (IPT) agreement 32,
   113–14
intellectual property (IP) 123
internet 41–4, 145–49
interoperability 94–5, 117, 138–39

JCT CE forms of contract 32, 114
Joint Contracts Tribunal (JCT) 18, 22

leadership 61–2, 80–1
legal frameworks 109–11
locating information 96–7

management process 85–7, 103–6
market conditions 21
metrics
     company 79–83
     individual 77–79
     information conventions 90–5
     processes 85–7
     project team 83–5
     roles and responsibilities 87
multi-disciplinary practices 59, 100
multiple offices 58–9

NEC3 contract 113–14

object associations 39–40
object libraries 38–40
office culture 79–80
office organisation and practice 59, 79–83
office size 57–9, 100, 106
on-demand software 46, 145
operational performance 128–130
outcomes 138–39

parametrics 40–1
PAS (Publicly Available Specification) 120–1
pilot projects 67–8, 102
Platform as a Service (PaaS) 45
policy drivers 133–4, 137
portals 41–3, 89
practice culture 79–80
practice size 57–9, 100, 106
procurement considerations 67–9
product information 73–5, 142–3
professional education 133–6
programme management 104
project life cycles 28–9
project teams 27–8, 83–5 (*see also* human
   resources; team working)
proprietary BIM (pBIM) 25
public sector clients 69–70, 119–31, 133–4

quality control 28, 104–5

research 139
RIBA Plan of Work 2013 124–6
risk management 106
roles and responsibilities 60, 87, 102,
   106–9, 124, 148–9

scale of business 57–9, 100, 106
search engines 144
security issues 147–9
semantic web 144, 149
service augmentation 64–5
skill levels 65–6, 107–8
small to medium sized enterprises (SMEs)
   22–3, 73
Soft Landings 128–30
Software as a Service (SaaS) 46

software platforms 88–90, 117–19, 141–2, 146
special interest groups 127–28
staffing *see* human resources
standards 46–9, 63, 81, 90–5, 138–9
Standards of Conduct and Practice 65–6
Strategic Forum for Construction 32, 113–14
strategic planning 103–4
supply chain 23, 73–7
system development 104
system management 107

team working 27–8, 32–3, 61–2, 82, 83–5, 141 (*see also* collaborative working)
training 54–6 (*see also* educational issues)

UK government policy 133–4, 137
UK government procurement 19, 21, 69–70, 119–31
Unified Classification for the Construction Industry (UNICLASS) 49, 63
US General Services Administration (GSA) 17, 67

value-added services 64–5
virtual agents 151–3
virtual information 146

whole life costs 139
work processes
    BIM 100–2, 104–5
    existing practices 59, 79–80, 83